Josef Hoffmann

Josef Hoffmann with one of his chairs, photographed in the studio of Kolo Moser
(ca. 1899)

Josef Hoffmann

Giuliano Gresleri

RIZZOLI
NEW YORK

First published in 1985 in the United States of America by
RIZZOLI INTERNATIONAL PUBLICATIONS, INC.
597 Fifth Avenue, New York, New York 10017

© 1981 Nicola Zanichelli S.p.A. Bologna, Italy

Library of Congress Cataloging in Publication Data

Gresleri, Giuliano.
    Josef Hoffmann.

    Translation of: Josef Hoffmann.
    Bibliography: p.
    1. Hoffmann, Josef Franz Maria, 1870–1956.
2. Architecture, Modern—20th century—Austria.
I. Title.
NA1011.5.H593G713   1985   720′.92′4   84-42749
ISBN 0-8478-0554-9 (pbk.)

Contents

Introduction

The Subversion of the Boudoir

. . . Small rooms, large rooms, dark rooms,
Rooms elegant and luminous with age.
I was searching for something—I didn't know what:
Not a study, not a workroom,
Not a living room; just a room
Someone had lived in before me,
The man I wanted to become.
—Robert Musil, 1903

The standard histories of modern architecture require that the leading figures and their work fall neatly on one side or the other of a readily identifiable watershed. This watershed, this critical yardstick, is the modern language of architecture, that manner of "speaking" defined by how much the architectural expression conforms to the supposedly clearly defined models from which the essence of any style emerges.

Yet rationalism, functionalism, organicism, and the very definition of the Modern Movement, presumably underwritten by a stable code of judgments and values, have by this time taken their place in a history composed of many histories and multiple truths. Intertwined in this web are forgotten figures and works, but certainly they are no less important to our story because they are not already among those in the acknowledged pantheon.

Recent research, particularly that which has been done with primary sources, has brought about a more complex—one might say more "honest"—reading of history. Figures who up to now have been seen as of minor importance in the history of design but who should have been given credit for their role in the development of the International Style are now revealed to be more ambiguous and infinitely richer than previously supposed. Others have emerged recently from a limbo which benevolently accepted them as "protagonists" up to a certain point, but ultimately considered them transgressors with respect to the general thesis; these figures now prove to us how much historical judgment calls for flexibility and attention to details and fragments—a method similar in substance to that of the archaeologist and the anthropologist.

Josef Hoffmann, along with Joseph Maria Olbrich, Adolf Loos, Otto Schönthal, Kolo Moser, and Gustav Klimt, was one of the leading figures in the artistic evolution of a Vienna that saw the close of a rich and highly developed cultural period and the beginnings of another no less rich or complex. He was one of those "great scorners," those men without qualities indispensable to a period of history which still seems to need updating and revision. To analyze the sources of this movement is not difficult. Hoffmann's work is as varied and heterogeneous as his culture, and as sophisticated and ambiguous as the period to which he belonged. It is more inclined to interpret than to direct or promote, to subvert without obviously asserting, to seek an isolation that allows it to carry to its extreme consequences, until all values are negated, the crisis of language that ultimately is Hoffmann's own crisis, that spoken of by Otto Wagner, by Friedrich Ohmann, by Carl von Hasenauer: the crisis of tradition. It is well known that the local tradition culminated with neoclassicism. Many commentators have stressed Gottfried Semper's immunity from the eclectic "contaminations" to which the rest of nineteenth-century European architecture was subject and how, at the same time, he succeeded in transmitting to a younger generation a manner rich in unsuspected possibilities.

Wagner himself after 1894, the year in which he was named professor at the Vienna Academy of Fine Arts, began promoting a radical renewal of the architectural language, proposing the necessity for a "morally" based architecture; however, he was not uncomfortable during the first thirty years of his professional activity and in his collaboration with Hasenauer in using a traditional repertory of forms which were already highly controversial in an international critical debate of far-reaching consequences. It would almost appear that in the Viennese context one need not discuss the general influence of traditional architectural figures, since the attention of the architects was already focused upon making small shifts away from this tradition—and these shifts, repeated systematically, would inevitably lead to the dissolution of the old system.

The idea of an artistic will, the basis of Alois Riegl's aesthetic theory, conferred on the artist the responsibility to intervene in the structural order of his society directly, interpreting its aspirations and endowing it with a "moral sense" that it would not otherwise have. This concept of individual action became, in the program of the avant-garde, a formative, polemical, and social obligation. When Wagner completed his *Moderne Architektur* for publication in 1895, he was preoccupied with making a theoretical distinction between the old and the modern and enunciating the terms of a modernity which henceforward would be clear and irrevocable; however, his language and points of reference still belong to a more established tradition of architecture. Only the desire for innovation separates it from traditional culture.[1] The same concepts of axiality, centrality, symmetry, functionality, and beauty are put into a simplified historical perspective that seems to want "to associate with the certainty of the collapse of a civilization the idea of a renewal of that same civilization, and to find among the ruins the indisputable conditions of beauty, the point where light will come out of darkness and bring about the reconciliation between man and industrial civilization."[2]

Wagner's faith, in a mythic age when "the revolution will be so violent that one will no longer be able to speak of a revival of the Renaissance," seems to imply a decisive renunciation of the formal complexity and heterogeneity of the nineteenth century, which justified its own stylistic plurality by the plurality of its contents. Yet the renewal of a style that would demonstrate that art from now on should transmit only "values" was not fulfilled in the brief span of years separating the eclectic tradition from the dawn of functionalism, and perhaps in reality was never fulfilled even later. The prophetic thirty years between 1890 and 1920, during which some of the most complex movements of modern architecture came into being and were concluded, saw the specters of a recent past coexist calmly with the disintegration of everyday life and the feverish activity of the avant-garde.

"The century that was in the process of being buried," writes Musil, "was not particularly distinguished during its second half. It was competent in technical matters, in business, and in scholarly pursuits, but outside of these domains, calm and false as stagnant water. Painting was like the old masters, writing like Goethe and Schiller, building in the Gothic and Renaissance style....From the stagnant water of the last two decades of the nineteenth century a kind of feverish winged creature arose and took flight all over Europe. No one knew exactly what was happening; no one could have predicted that a new art, a new morality, or a new social order was in the making. But everyone described what it looked like. And everywhere there were people who were opposed to this nonsense."[3]

Within this climate, and because of the widespread desire to find a moral basis for design—a desire ultimately traceable to William Morris—and to create a "true and proper" style that derived from its own time and embraced all the arts, Hoffmann's contribution to the development of modern architecture seems disquieting and difficult to assess within the established framework. It is a body of work that belongs to a climate of general precariousness, one in which the values of the sign, of materials, and of surfaces are investigated with a scientific and irreverent curiosity altogether unknown to the Modern Movement. Hoffmann's work has in Gustav Klimt and later in Paul Klee its natural points of reference and significant echoes.

Angels and Acroteria in Vienna; Humble Spirits on the Hohe Warte

In 1895 the magazine *Der Architekt* published with some fanfare the project Hoffmann had submitted to the *Prix de Rome* jury: a complex of buildings making up a colossal mausoleum dedicated to the celebration of peace. Although obviously eclectic in its derivation, the work clearly alludes to the Opera of Charles Garnier and to the manner of Gottfried Semper. However, if we compare the project with Hoffmann's studio work of the preceding years, now housed in the Picture Archives of the Austrian National Library, we can easily see the degree of maturity achieved by this pupil of Otto Wagner. The caryatids, columns, and angels that crown the roofs and tympanums of vernacular public buildings here become details of a composition that directly recalls Semper's project for the Forum of Dresden, while the great column of the Winged Victory not only evokes Trajan's Column but also Wagner's work at its most classical.[4]

It is a composition of fragments, in substance, assembled in the established tradition of the eclectic school. However, when one looks more closely, one sees that the elements do not simply amount to a "mixed bag": the profusion of angels and acroteria atop every vertical element transform the classical Wagnerian reference into a parody. Even the central cupola of the temple of peace does not culminate in the canonical manner; the lantern blossoms into a balloon-like metal bulb, architecturally exaggerated by the footing that supports it. It is a singular anticipation of the symbolic dome of gilt leaves placed by Olbrich on the roof of the Secession building, as well as of the figures by Franz Metzner surrounding the tower of the Palais Stoclet. An extravagant, amusing project, the rhetoric of the whole ensemble gives way to an obvious irony that seems to mock every manner and invert the rational order of reality, as in the geometric little grove of oranges placed on top of the caisson at the base of the piers of the bridge. But there is something more: in the almost casually juxtaposed forms, there is a spatiality which is colossal but also traditional; past and present coexist in this irreverent project. Up to this moment, Hoffmann liked to think of himself above all as a continuer of the tradition, even a reviver of it; his mistrust of an avant-garde of any tendency or stripe prevented him from committing its easy errors, but also, in the long run, from escaping a too restrictive point of view.

Hoffmann's experience of the classical models, already broadly explored in exotic sources such as the Oriental and late-Roman models to which his curiosity led him between 1890 and 1900, did not seem to exhaust itself prior to his trip to Italy, which provided him with the possibility for a general rethinking of the very significance of "architecture."

"Let us also cast a glance at that time when people asked of the art of construction only protection from the natural elements. Here may be found the first traces of the carefree architecture of the East."[5] Olbrich's brief recommendation, written on the back of a postcard sent from Capri, only served to confirm interests that were being defined in those years when Wagner was urging his students to return architecture to its primary sources. "Man's first motivation and his original purpose for building was certainly the need to protect himself from the weather, from his fellow men, and from wild animals. The seeds of architecture lie in construction ... as well as in simple utility. But this was not enough, for man's sense of beauty called for art and required that it be made part of the building. Thus architecture was born."[6] These axioms signal Hoffmann's and Olbrich's primary interest in the house as a *dwelling*, a theme common to their work following their return from Italy to Vienna, a time when they were associated with Wagner in working on the Vienna subway system, and then during the convivial meetings of the *Siebener Club*, a group whose founding in the midst of a climate of increasing national feeling indicated the birth of a concept of art as the product of a collective will.

From the city to the individual house, Wagner's pupils then paradoxically overturned the objectives of their master. The *Heimatstil*, towards which Josef August Lux pushed Hoffmann in the pages of his newspaper *Hohe Warte*, implies not only the avowed desire to return to nature which was common to all of the Secession group, but a subtler necessity, a thinly concealed desire to return to the symbolic and sublime womb of Mother Austria. One can see this desire as another face of the unreal Celtic dream of Lethaby's *Architecture, Mysticism and Myth*,[7] a book whose influence on the atmosphere surrounding *Ver Sacrum* makes it easy to grasp how much the Viennese movement owed to the ornate robe in which William Morris dressed his wife in his painting of her as Queen Guinevere.[8]

At that time the Secession had little import; one spoke of *Heimatstil* and *Heimatkünstler*, a concept of native styles and homespun artists that would become increasingly suspect as Vienna approached its twilight. Moreover, the first act of these revolutionaries was exquisitely institutional, the founding of the *Vereinigung der bildenden Künstler Österreichs*, which celebrated itself in Olbrich's Secession building, flamboyantly alluding to Voyseyan ideas which had been imported by von Scala in the exhibition at the Museum of Art and Industry, and holding a fascination which even the sober-minded Emperor himself did not know how to escape.[9]

While the temple of the "royalists" of the Secession group rose, thus, two steps away from the temple of the "orthodox" of the Künstlerhaus in front of the Karlskirche, the *Vereinigung* celebrated the rites of domestic architecture on the edge of the Vienna Woods. Here, on the Hohe Warte, a pleasant suburb of the capital, Hoffmann replaced Olbrich, who had moved to Darmstadt, as the architect of an intellectual elite destined to determine the course of Viennese events for more than thirty years to come.

The Orientalism of Olbrich, who set himself apart by his meditations on Klimt's work and by his Greco-Egyptian allusions in the Friedman House, no longer affected Hoffmann's more tranquil work. The experience of the Hohe Warte above all served Hoffmann as a complex laboratory for applied art, characterized by a precise desire to refine further and further. He assimilated the language of the Glasgow School, ultimately going radically beyond it by virtue of an intellectual theory that embraced— perhaps without being critical enough—the theory of the total work of art.

None of the houses designed by Hoffmann along what would become the most famous street of this Viennese suburb succeeded in translating the transparent clarity of the projects, drawings, and graphics of *Ver Sacrum* into built form. The architecture did not effect the celebration of the "void" nor the magic spell of "absence" pursued, for example, by Adolf Böhm. The houses of the Hohe Warte, despite the surprising roof detail of the Villa Moll, seem almost to contradict what one might have anticipated from Hoffmann on the basis of his *intérieurs*. The Moser, Spitzer, and Henneberg houses, all built within a single span of time, at times simultaneously, are the product of calm practice, of unimpeded research into a style. Concerned with the problems of compositional fragmentation and formal relationships he saw in the English models, Hoffmann employed a style of drawing that follows the vision of Voysey and Baillie Scott without being slavish to it.

If the spatial picture that emerges of the Hohe Warte does not appear especially innovative compared to its Anglo-Saxon precedents, it was nevertheless during this period that Hoffmann translated into architectural terms—as Rochowanski recounts having heard from the master himself—the entire iconography of the Sacred Spring. Thus, in every garden of the Hohe Warte, as in his own aristocratic family house in Pirnitz, there was "...a path to the castle and a small park where one may dream, the rarest of trees...a whimsical gazebo and a small lake with a little island in the middle...and boats in summer."[10]

But the Hohe Warte on the edge of the Wiener Wald was not the place where Queen Guinevere and her famous robe would be embodied; the space and form of her boudoir were still too orthodox. It was in the magic white, lilac, and rose interior created by Charles Rennie Mackintosh for Fritz Warndörfer that the seeds of a subtle subversion of the Viennese aristocracy were first planted. The Secession too would have its secessionists.

From Purkersdorf to Brussels: the Vicissitudes of the Fantasy

The three years between the founding of the Wiener Werkstätte in 1902 and the disbanding of the original Secession group (Wagner, Klimt, Moser, Hoffmann, Moll, Luksch) saw Hoffmann busy with the installations for the Werkstätte exhibitions.

The experience of the Hohe Warte ended with the spectacular solutions for the furnishing of the Villa Spitzer. The "English manner" here is decisively dissolved into a casual, illogical spatiality, manifested on white plaster surfaces whose geometry, instead of defining volumes, plays itself out in its own articulation and framing. The lighting fixtures hang from the ceiling like "architectural machines," making the space around them read as juxtaposed and layered planes. Nevertheless everything appears to occupy its place by chance, as in a house of cards where one has only to touch one element to cause the destruction of the whole thing. The main hall of the Villa Spitzer, the epitome of all this, presents itself as a clean break with previous interiors, but it is also the point of departure for a new tendency to celebrate and monumentalize the space of the house.

Whether one considers it a sanatorium with its associated buildings or the richest of bourgeois houses of the time, in the Palais Stoclet the representational power of the space is expressed with ostentatious confidence. The result, first worked out in a fragmentary series of solutions, is a product of style, school, and "manner." It is obtained here solely through the use of a clear language comprehensible to all, resounding with history and tradition. That Hoffmann consciously turned during these years to the works of that "new path" charted by Wagner after 1898 in his Majolica House with its faience facade seems to be demonstrated by the fact that he shows little interest in modern materials.[11]

On the other hand, recent studies make it clear that the "classical mode of expression" of which Frampton speaks, although correct within the context of the author's thesis, ought to be approached with extreme caution.[12] The works that illustrate what only for the sake of convenience might be called Hoffmann's "new interests" are the interiors of the Klinger Room at the XIVth exhibition of the Secession (1902), the installations for the Wiener Werkstätte pavilion in Düsseldorf (1903), and the interiors for the Wiener Werkstätte exhibition in Vienna (1904).

Hoffmann's 1902 installation in Olbrich's Secession building of Max Klinger's sculpture of Beethoven and Klimt's frieze was "graphicized" to become the classic frontispiece of *Ver Sacrum*. Just as a false pilaster that functions as a typographic frieze closes the symmetrical plan of the building and pulls one's attention away from the center of the space, so Hoffmann's installation contradicted the very sense of

Olbrich's design, which ought to have been the exaltation of a single focal point. "The whole building was transformed," writes Werner Hoffmann. "The main gallery was dominated by a spectacular sculpture, the *leitmotiv* of a three-dimensional 'symphony' whose symbolic and decorative 'movements' were distributed all around the room. This exhibition gave the Secession members an opportunity to prove their versatility as artisans as well as their talent for improvisation."

To the classicism of the plan corresponds, then, a "symbolic" and more random reading of the space. The architectural axis from the entry to the monument is contradicted by the elaborate path which the visitor must follow; he clearly knows where the object of his curiosity is located, but that same object is continually denied him, accessible only after he passes through shadowy areas where friezes, furniture, winged figures winking at him from a twilight zone, masks, and totems make up the mystical procession of the Sacred Spring. It is the epitome of the idea of the pavilion-temple (basilica plan with niches and altars), the sacred place of the culture of an elite, the container of the unique art of an entire nation and celebration of that nation.

To all this the 1903 pavilion in Düsseldorf adds the ingredient of the exotic: the circulation paths converge on a small room with an exedra and fountain, where there is a frieze of geishas making sacrifices to Spring. There are still evocations of the Orient and the Mediterranean, of spring as the primeval season. The overflowing desire to recall images of an abandoned sunlight calls forth a need for dignity and composure. Pilasters, niches, and apses remain the iconographic devices of a composition that alludes to classicism, but it is a classicism continually contradicted by the decorative use of those very elements. No element is more important than any other, but together they make for a vibrant surface, the very apotheosis of the flat plane and the negation of every traditional meaning of perspectival space. In this atmosphere, all forms seem magically suspended in an empty space like that which Klimt proposed in his University frescoes.[13]

It is in the sanatorium at Purkersdorf that there are suggestions of a style to come—perhaps European functionalism; it thus represents the arrival point of an exuberant, unusually inventive, and highly personal search. The astonishing interior, executed a year after the Wiener Werkstätte exhibition, is an apparently casual assemblage drawing on every known building type but reduced according to the usual process of simplification to only the memory of itself. What is born from this conscious desire to remake, repropose, retell by subverting all accepted linguistic rules, is the very style that later will be called "the style of Hoffmann." At the heart of this discourse, the compositional elements—walls, columns, cornices, partitions, apses, niches, tympanums—are not so much subordinate parts of the whole; they themselves are the "architecture." They can be isolated and enlarged to the scale of a giant order (Purkersdorf, for example, is none other than the famous cabinet of 1901 blown up to the dimensions of a building), or reduced to the size of knick-knacks (as in the series of temple pendants produced by the Wiener Werkstätte during these years), but they always remain themselves: architectural objects *par excellence*.

On the heels of this new direction, the Palais Stoclet may certainly be considered an anomaly (especially in view of its extraordinary program), but more than the sum and apotheosis of the style of Hoffmann, as it is always seen, it is the concrete expression of a design strategy brought to the highest level of execution. Palais Stoclet synthesizes the preceding works leading up to it, as well as anticipates the subsequent ones that are indebted to it. More amenable than the improbable hermeticism of Purkersdorf, more complex than any work he had previously conceived, the building, in all its extravagance, is that unique work that hovers in the mind of every architect until the moment it can finally be realized. The monumental scale and the materials, the unusual spatial inventions that upset all traditional logic (the exterior marble cladding with bronze moldings along the cornices, the even more precious cut pieces of marble used in the interiors), and the amusing, deliberate desire to adhere to the wishes of the client while eluding them give the building a strange reality. They destine it to take its place in the list of important modern buildings arousing in the viewer that typical discomfort reserved for works that depart from accepted rules.

Still more than at Purkersdorf all the ingredients of an "academic" architectural composition are employed here: the monumental and ceremonial porticoed entry, the observation tower, apses, tympanums, and columns, bridges striding across the garden, fountains and exedrae, niches and balconies. Everything is grotesquely giganticized or miniaturized, everything knowingly subverted by the complexity of spatial relations. All is then controlled by a classical sense of calm, giving the whole a hierarchical order. Intruding upon the clear arrangement of the landscaped Pompeian garden, the architecture appears to be constructed out of the "rationalized naturalness" of its exterior surrounds. This naturalness is brought back into the material dimensions of the built work to give meaning to its precise contents, as in the standing figure of Athena on top of the entry vestibule and the statues of Hercules on the crowning tower.

A temple of beauty and wealth, the Palais Stoclet nevertheless remains an enigma. Built to exalt the values of a world rapidly moving toward a destiny it could not have imagined, it remains in the history of architecture as the last of the great ceremonial buildings, and one of the first of a new tendency lacking an apparent relationship to the past. Its immense spaces are not filled with footsteps, speech, laughter; instead every day a comedy of happiness, power, and opulence is played out. As at one of Paul Poiret's famous banquets, every evening Madame Stoclet-Stevens (dressed as an Assyrian in Klimt's well-known frieze in the dining room) descends the staircase of the great hall under the ecstatic eyes of the European intelligentsia, dressed in a silver robe: an ultimate homage to the spirit of Queen Guinevere.

Space without Dimensions and Men without Quality

Hoffmann returned to the Hohe Warte after ten years to build the Villa Ast. Levetus, presenting it in *Moderne Bauformen* after it was completed, called it the apotheosis of the tradition, "the very document of the new Viennese style."[14] In his rhetorical and aestheticizing description, however, there emerges a barely concealed discomfort in ascertaining how this new work fits into the supposedly established evolution of Hoffmann's work: the "differences" with respect to the Palais Stoclet, which was still in the process of completion, are obvious; with respect to Purkersdorf, they are troubling; while with respect to the other houses of the Hohe Warte, the conception seems entirely contradictory.

Levetus did not find it easier—as did a number of later critics—to pass quickly over the exterior of the building. He was troubled by the fact that the work exhibited the full repertory of fragile figurative elements in the famous Wiener Werkstätte vocabulary, but that paradoxically it was built of concrete, as an assemblage of discrete, juxtaposed elements, "...from the cornices to the monumental containers for flowers in the garden." His discomfort was justified. The architecture is still conceived as an object, but in Brussels it was extroverted, a deliberate attempt to create a unity with the designed exterior context. Here the house is introverted, and instead of the excessive refinement of detail the material is rough and handcrafted. The jewelbox house, the "transparent" dwelling, is now closed like a strongbox. Inside, the preciousness of yellow Lonneller marble, white Laaser marble with gilt edging, gray-white *cipollino* marble, and Makassar wood furnishings structure a space around Klimt's paintings, *The Danae* and *The Sisters*, a space proportioned to the art, without any functional relation to the logic of the house. The vista that floats into the main hall upon entry takes in the living room, Mrs. Ast's boudoir, and the dining room, which opens toward the veranda and the mock swimming pool, half water and half grass, circumscribed by a unique scroll-shaped border later admired by van Ravesteyn.

The gilded and "empty" interior realm behind the exterior walls of the site is cold, massive, and inarticulate despite the profuse decoration. The pilasters with their excessive fluting become colossal at the corners, and are cut in an arbitrary fashion by the heavy crown of the cornice line, ornamented with motifs even more complex than those used in the Palais Stoclet. The idea of a coloration without color, of a monumentality without weight, and of a unity composed of autonomous spatial parts subtends Hoffmann's desire to undermine every certainty and to leave suspended every definitive judgment on his work. But the apparent contradictions are simply an aspect of their harmonious accord: everything can change in the brief course of a day, every architectural object has an independent existence, defines and redefines itself. The entire house, apparently thought out for all eternity, is only made to last a moment. Every hour is different, just as in Hoffmann's plans for the garden, which Herr Ast was obliged to change with each new season according to the light, color, and weather.

Is the building a monument to capitalism, to its logic and its possibilities? Certainly, but it is also a celebration of the idea of dwelling, an exaltation of values shifting in the extreme attempt to recover a language that the avant-garde condemned because it was antithetical to their program. The Villa Ast, on which the Wiener Werkstätte worked for more than three years, is a concrete meditation on the theme of the house, and it is diametrically opposed to contemporary European work on the theme of housing. It and its more modest variations—from the small houses of the colony in Kaasgraben and the second Ast house on the Wörthersee, up to the more complex undertakings of the Villa Primavesi and the house for Sonia Knips—reflect the powerful richness of Hoffmann's work. The will to contradict an academic classicism incontrovertibly by, however, using a language of forms that is recognizable, immediately identifiable within the formal code of the tradition and the figurative repertory of the local culture as well as that of Greece, Byzantium, and Ravenna, opens a chapter in the history of modern architecture which is to be as discontinuous and fragmented as the world in which it was written.

Ten years later, the Villa Ast would appear very far away, like Heckel's contemporary painting *Pheasant Castle*—irretrievable even for Hoffmann himself, an apparition from the past. In a certain sense, Hoffmann's career here has a beginning and an end. Villa Ast is the touchstone, the forebear, of a generation of objects that is constantly revisited, from the pavilion in Rome that served as Austria's temple at the exposition of 1911 to the one for Paris of 1925. Memories, spatial echoes, and materials carrying unfamiliar messages are reflected from one work to the next, each work graspable to the extent that it opens itself up to different architectural languages.

The partially "moral" judgment that even recently has been passed on the work of Hoffmann does not take into account this cultural diversity born out of the complexity of the historical moment and the specific place in which it took form. "In contrast to Adolf Loos," notes Friedrich Achleitner, "Josef Hoffmann did not see (or because of his own talents and ambitions did not want to see) the historical logic of this development. He made the ultimate response to the grandiose demands of the dying Austrian monarchy. While Loos recognized the problems and tasks of a social architecture without seeking a formal solution to them, the late works of Hoffmann once again take up the presumptions of a decadent nobility."[15]

Today we know that this type of judgment is always formulated more from an ideological view of history than from an analysis of its contents. From the roofs of the cubical *Höfe* to the cornice lines of the more modest *Landhaus* designed in the thirties, and even when the language and atmosphere of Vienna are replaced by that of an international academy (under the interested encouragement of Hoffmann's young disciples), the repeated and varied, accidental or deliberate motifs of the pitched roof, the tympanum, and the acroteria provocatively remain the archetypal signs of Hoffmann's work.

The theme of the dwelling is taken up again and again, but the reference becomes ever more fleeting, until it finally disappears in the cages containing the stairs of the Werkbundsiedlung housing of 1932. The disorientation that we experience today before the cold, stiff, and sad facade of the Austrian Pavilion for the Venice Biennale of 1934 is a symptom of our own incapacity to read history deeply, our own refusal to listen to its last words. The epoch of caryatids and angels was interrupted by international developments that favored a lack of imagination. The house, as in the famous Expressionist film of Stellan Rye, often seemed to be "a house without doors and windows," a building stripped, that is, of the elements essential to it. One might say of it, as actor Asta Nielsen did in 1913, "...Millions of men admired me, but I alone know at what expense. Do you see now why I have a sad face?"

1. Otto Wagner, *Moderne Architektur. Seinen Schülern ein Führer auf diesem Kunstgebiete* (Vienna, 1895).
2. Henry van de Velde, *Formules de la Beauté architectonique moderne* (Weimar, 1916–1917). This quotation is discussed in the introduction by Anne Lambrichs and Maurice Culot to the Italian edition, *Formule della Bellezza architettonica moderna* (Bologna: Zanichelli, 1981).
3. Robert Musil, *Der Mann ohne Eigenschaften* (Vienna, 1930).
4. See in particular several projects executed by Otto Wagner around 1880, among them the Artibus, a fantastical and grandiose complex dedicated to the cult of art, which would have been built on the banks of an artificial lake and in which there are quotations from Semper and Schinkel. Other sources for Hoffmann's project may be found in Wagner's competition drawings for the Budapest Parliament of 1882.
5. Olbrich's letter is quoted by Eduard Sekler in his essay "Il viaggio in Italia di Olbrich e Hoffmann," in the exhibition catalogue *Artisti austriaci a Roma* (Rome, 1972).
6. Wagner, *Moderne Architektur*, op. cit.
7. *Architecture, Mysticism and Myth* is the title of the well-known book by William Lethaby in which the idea of a symbolic architecture is rooted in Celtic culture as the basis for a national language; the argument comes out of the English tradition of romantic socialism. The text establishes the continuity between its own thesis and the more pragmatic tendencies of the Arts and Crafts.
8. Before immersing himself in the study of the Arthurian legend and English utopism, Morris painted *Queen Guinevere*, the only easel painting that is definitely attributable to him. It hangs today in the Tate Gallery in London. A portrait of his wife, Jane Burden, in an idealized Pre-Raphaelite interior, *Queen Guinevere* was considered by the circle around Morris' firm of Morris, Marshall, Faulkner & Co. to be the emblem of a return to Celtic myth in art and to handicrafts as the New Free Style expression of national cultural identity.

9. The History Archives in Vienna possess many photographs of this particular event, among which is a rather well known one portraying Franz Joseph and his dignitaries with the artists of the Secession.

10. L. W. Rochowanski, *Josef Hoffmann* (Vienna: Verlag der Österreichischen Staatsdruckerei, 1950), p.15.

11. Cf. Kenneth Frampton, *Modern Architecture: A Critical History* (London: Oxford, 1980), p.81.

12. I am referring especially to Francesco Cellini's essay "La Villa Ast di Josef Hoffmann," in *Controspazio*, June 1977. This is the first critical work to propose an alternative reading of Hoffmann's work at the time of the Villa Ast.

13. Between 1900 and 1902, prior to his trip to Ravenna, Gustav Klimt obtained the commission to execute an allegory of Medicine, Law, and Philosophy for the University of Vienna. The figures have inspired comments about their "suspension in a flattened space," their reduction to a single dimension, and the total absence of all perspectival representation.

14. A. S. Levetus, "Villa Ast," in *Moderne Bauformen*, February 1924.

15. F. Achleitner, "L'Österreichischer Werkbund e i suoi rapporti col Deutscher Werkbund," in *Werkbund, Germania, Austria, Svizzera*, edited by L. Burckardt (Venice: La Biennale di Venezia, 1977).

Acknowledgments

This book would not have been possible without the help of friends and collaborators. I am particularly grateful to Franco Fornatti, docent at the Schillerplatz Academy, for his constant availability to me; to Umberto Tasca and Paolo Gresleri, who intelligently photographed many of the buildings; and to Maria Grazia, who read the text with her customary attentiveness.

Projects

Myth, Handicraft, and the Sacred Spring

1892   Mausoleum for Art Exhibitions

This is one of Hoffmann's many early designs made while he was enrolled in the Akademie der bildenden Künste (the Academy of Fine Arts). Carl von Hasenauer, who was then building the Burgtheater, was the director of studies at the academy, and encouraged his students' monumental fancies. This project for a large temple for art exhibitions is a theme which would reappear frequently in Hoffmann's work. The drawing is one of a series made in a graphic style unusual for this period, falling between romanticism and the work of Schinkel, as well as recalling the work of Charles Chipiez. One sees Hoffmann's early interest in a Roman-Oriental style. The building is completely self-sufficient, independent of the medieval city suggested in the background; detaching itself from the old, the building rises in steep stairs to the new heavens of art, a Tower of Babel embracing all languages.

1895

Forum Orbis–Insula Pacis

Forum of the World—Island of Peace

Like Olbrich, who won the prize two years earlier, Hoffmann also used his *prix de Rome* project—the Forum Orbis—as the basis for the honors thesis he later completed under Otto Wagner. Wagner had this year issued his "lecture course" *Moderne Architektur,* published by Schroll, for the benefit of the students at the academy, where he had replaced Carl von Hasenauer.

The Forum Orbis clearly shows a compositional skill that displays a technical mastery and intimate knowledge of historical models such as Sacconi's monument to Victor Emmanuel II in Rome and Semper and Hasenauer's work on the Burgtheater in Vienna.

It seems that Hoffmann sought to "dilute" the experiences of his masters and teachers into an excessive and convoluted manner that ended up in a parody of their style. Camouflaged in the complexity of the composition are details which seem ironic in the rhetorical context of the project, such as the numerous acroteria and the unexpected group of orange trees planted on the pier of the bridge.

Main elevation

Side view with the commemorative colonnade and the suspension bridge

1896   The Trip to Italy

Rome: head of a lady

"I too have been in Arcadia"

The traditional grand tour took Hoffmann through Italy on more or less the same itinerary as that followed by Olbrich two years earlier. However, while Olbrich went on to the extravagant exoticism of North Africa, Hoffmann preferred to remain in the Roman ambience of Pompeii and Pozzuoli. There are about 200 well-known drawings from this trip, including a large number of Roman and Neapolitan subjects.

Unlike Olbrich's experiences, Hoffmann's impressions of his trip derived primarily from examples of vernacular architecture. Some designs appeared later as illustrations in *Der Architekt,* while others appeared in *Ver Sacrum* with a commentary by Adolf Loos. They reveal the movement of Hoffmann's interest beyond the architecture of the Mediterranean myth. The subjects he drew indicate his preference for analyzing simple aggregate structures and volumetric and formal information, showing his independence of the pressure of the academy to document only the great classical works of architecture. The drawings also show his fascination with the symbolic meaning of the house in the landscape, with the residence as an archetype, and his attempt to capture its functional mechanism, the very essence of its architectural specificity, which derives from its geographic location and its cultural influences.

It is interesting to note how a view of a house in Posillipo built on a steeply sloping grade subsequently reappears in a design for a proposal for terraced villas. In a recent essay Eduard Sekler has shown the transformation of this source in the Böhler House on the outskirts of Vienna, built in 1909.

On April 21, 1894, Olbrich had written to Hoffmann from Benevento: "The old ruins teach us mainly three things: that the architects built them out of a sense of beauty, fantasy, and taste; and to this they added a decisive sense of the practical and functional."

House in southern Italy

Rome, tomb on top of
the wall of the Villa
of the Knights of Malta

Farmhouse with terraces

House stepped down
to the bay of Pozzuoli,
with a sketch of a villa

1899–1900 The Exotic Orient

The interior designs of Baillie-Scott and the bamboo and majolica furniture which was popular in Vienna at the beginning of the century were not the only indications of the keen local interest in the exotic during this period. In literature and later in Alois Riegl's aesthetic theories the same tendency was pursued, while the Imperial collections were brimming with chinoiserie. In England, Repton had planned his pavilion in Brighton in the Indian style in 1808, Brodrick designed the baths in Leeds in a Moorish style in 1840, and Decker's *Chinese Architecture* had a new success. In Corfu, the interior of King George I's royal palace was furnished with exceptional Chinese works, and the collections in Franz Joseph's hunting lodge were impressive.

The Bildarchiv in Vienna now contains Hoffmann's designs and sketches of Oriental subjects, taken from books, pictures, and prints of the period, and this interest of Hoffmann's coincides for a time with the graphic work of *Ver Sacrum.* Josef Maria Auchentaller and Max Benirschke on the one hand and Adolf Böhm and Hoffmann on the other transcribed the delicate dreams of Bearsdley and Baillie-Scott. But above all, it is in issue nine of its second series that *Ver Sacrum* used the Oriental motif extensively. The cover was drawn in the Japanese style, and the issue was compiled for the occasion of the VIth

Interior designs for
Das Interieur, ca. 1901

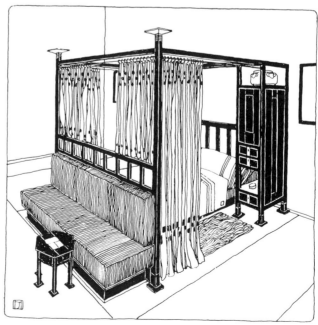

Study sketch of a pagoda near Kyoto

Secession Exhibition, which contained the print collection
Adolf Fischer had brought from Japan. For the exhibition,
highly popular with the Viennese artists, Fischer had also
produced a small introductory catalogue.

From the beginning, the Secession exhibitions were
filled with pagodas, irises, roses, and chrysanthemums.
After 1900, these also frequently appeared in the gardens
of Hoffmann's houses, as they had at the Collalto Castle
and in the fantastic garden of his family house in Pirnitz,
Moravia.

1898–1900   Objects and Forms of the Sacred Spring

"Red currants, mauve flowers, and wild strawberries"

Bearded and prophetlike, Hermann Bahr announced the beginning of a new flowering in the arts to the students of the Academy. The Secession journal, *Ver Sacrum,* was first published in January 1898, with an introduction by Max Burckardt, director of the Burgtheater. For five years, the magazine disseminated the "Viennese style" throughout the world. The hibiscus, designed by Alfred Roller for the first cover of *Ver Sacrum,* breaks with its roots from its old container, and Arno Holz sings to the rosy goddess Aurora: " . . . Blau blitzt das Meer, ich bin ein Grieche . . . " (" . . . Blue gleams the sea, I am a Greek . . . ").

Hoffmann published sketches and projects in this journal: country houses immersed perspectively in a precise spatial context, fragments of temples dedicated to the cult of art, in the manner of Olbrich. Hoffman built the latter in concrete at his first opportunity, as may be seen in the Apollo Store.

Country house, 1898

Idea for a building dedicated to the arts, 1898

Architectural study, 1898

1898

Furnishings for
the Editorial Offices
of *Ver Sacrum*

Vienna

This is a work of minor importance, but it is significant for understanding the meaning of Hoffmann's experiments in the genre of the *intérieur*. As much as the Ver Sacrum *Zimmer* may still be indebted to the manner of Kolo Moser, an influence not to be overlooked, one can recognize Hoffmann's overriding interest in the work of Olbrich, especially in the two portals of the room. Hoffmann is clearly telling us that a room is nothing but a geometric space determined by the meeting of twelve lines (which he emphasizes by placing the wood corners in relief) and neutral areas of plaster.

≡ VER SACRUM-ZIMMER. ≡
ENTWORFEN VON JOSEF
HOFFMANN. O. M.

1898–1918 Secretary's Office for the Secession

Vienna

In this building, designed by Olbrich and finished in six months at the end of 1898, Hoffmann decorated the secretary's office and some of the other rooms. These spaces are even more contained than those of the Ver Sacrum *Zimmer,* but they are expanded by the singular presence of pieces of furniture which have lost their functional identity. Bookshelves and showcases assume the unusual forms of a newly invented rationality, which contrasts with the profuse floral decoration painted on the walls. The very free arrangement of the furniture, off-axis and on the diagonal, is unique for an architect who would soon give every object in his houses a precise space, fixed forever.

1902

Villa Henneberg
on the Hohe Warte

Vienna

Hugo Henneberg, a photographer and collector of Japanese prints and a frequent member of the circle of followers around the Secession, was among the group of clients who wished to establish a residential colony on the Hohe Warte. This project had earlier been entrusted to Olbrich, but after his departure for Darmstadt, between 1902 and 1903, the contract was given to Hoffmann, who built four famous villas there. The plans and elevations especially reveal Hoffmann's deliberate intention to move beyond the early iconography of the Secession.

The dimensions of the rooms are reduced to make space for the large *Halle*, clearly a reference to Mackintosh's design for the library of the Glasgow School of Art.

It must not be forgotten, in this context, that Mackintosh had been engaged by the Secession to plan the interior decoration of an entire room at the Secession exhibition of 1900, a design which Hoffman studied in depth.

In the double-height space of the Henneberg house, Hoffmann sums up the very meaning of the new domestic space, filling it with furniture by Moser, Mackintosh, and himself, and several large paintings by Klimt. The elevations in particular are the result of an intentional stylistic simplification, seen in the extensive use of the black and white checkered wall panels, even though this intention was partly sacrificed in the actual construction of the house.

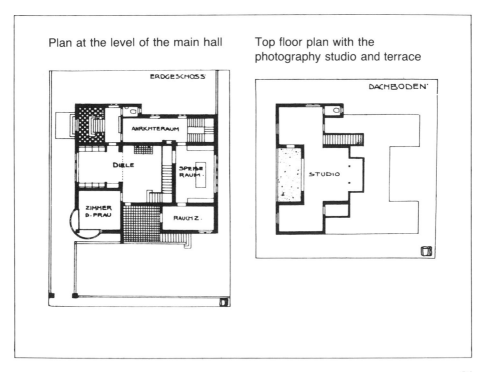

Plan at the level of the main hall

Top floor plan with the photography studio and terrace

West elevation

North elevation

Section

South elevation

33

1902–1903 Villa Moll on the Hohe Warte

Steinfeldgasse 6, Vienna XIX

More monumental and rambling than the others, the Villa Moll appears even today, despite the extensive alterations, to be a unique combination of English and Secession themes, intermingled with elements of a constantly evoked *Heimatstil*. The extraordinary "event" of the pyramidal and windowed central volume, whose pitched roof at one time was supported by curved iron corbels, remains an anomalous episode in Hoffmann's iconography. Olbrich had crowned the towers of his exhibition building on the Mathildenhöhe with similar forms, but he used them as part of a compositional logic that appeared "natural." Here, Hoffmann obviously wished to introduce an anomalous element within an "acceptable" structure, thereby facilitating the endorsement of this new device. The villa's entire garden was arranged with seasonal hothouse plants and trees, and with what would later become Hoffmann's typical fountain, all indications of an "architecture of the ephemeral" which he would develop extensively. The house pleased Carl Moll enormously, and his painting of it is now in the Albertina Museum in Vienna.

The villa today

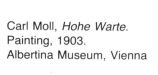

Carl Moll, *Hohe Warte*.
Painting, 1903.
Albertina Museum, Vienna

The facade as it was in 1903 before adjacent constructions

View from the garden

1902–1903 Villa Spitzer on the Hohe Warte

Steinfeldgasse 4, Vienna XIX

The last villa to be built for Hoffmann's Secession friends, the Villa Spitzer has been the most consistently admired of the three completed in 1903. Dr. Spitzer's villa, although in many respects like the others, was described by Hoffmann's contemporaries as a "tale of glass," most likely alluding to the "transparency" of its facades. Here, Hoffmann indicated the future characteristics of his architecture: large interior wall areas plastered white, strongly framed by walnut woodwork, service area flooring in black and white checks, a precise arrangement of white lacquered furniture placed against a white background, and illumination by ceiling lamps that function as architectural objects demanding their own space. The Villa Spitzer was the fruit of long and careful work, from plan to realization. A collective product in the sense that it was influenced by the work of many Secession artists, the material fact of the architecture speaks for itself. The hand of the master emerges once again as the great protagonist.

The main hall

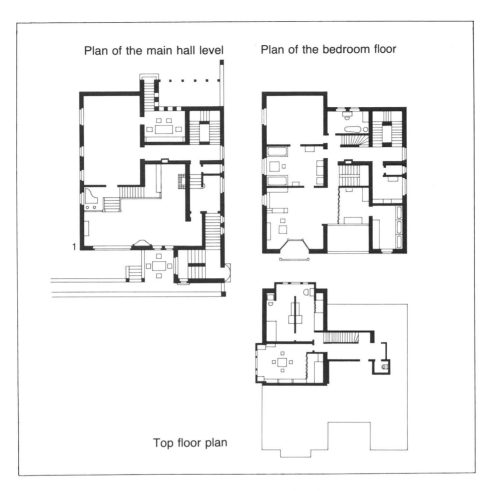

Plan of the main hall level

Plan of the bedroom floor

Top floor plan

East elevation

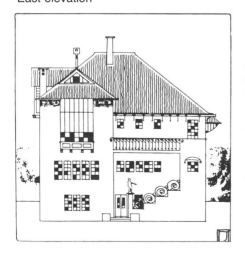

South elevation

SÜDSEITE

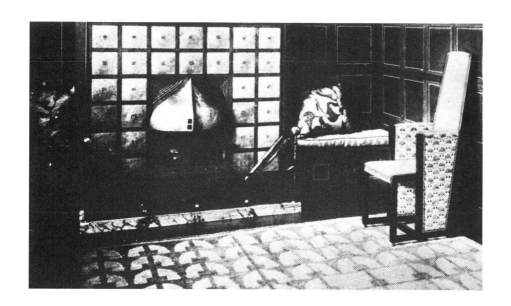

The gas fireplace in the hall

Spitzer's studio as seen in a photograph of the period

First floor office

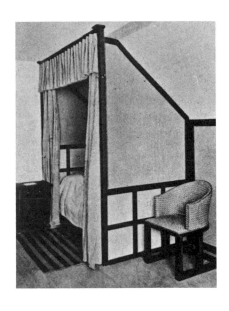

Bedroom

Light fixture

Detail of the furnishing

1902

Klinger Room at the XIVth Secession Exhibition

Vienna

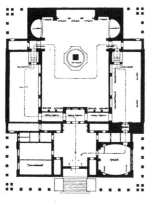

Plan of the Secession Building after Hoffmann's interventions

The furnishings which Hoffman continuously produced for the buildings of the Secession reached an exceptional complexity in his work for the XIVth Secession Exhibition. Many critics justifiably begin with this work in their analysis of Hoffmann's architecture, considering it to have more significance and content than his earlier works. The rigidity of Olbrich's plan is broken up by a series of independent, casually arranged spaces, connected by the logic of a circulation route culminating in Klinger's statue of Beethoven and the frieze in which Klimt engraved his refined geometrical design in gold leaf on plaster, a technique derived from the local vernacular. The entire pavilion is filled with forms which contradict the very concept of "interior decoration," for they are endowed with their own architecture monumentality, taking up the celebratory motif in decorative portals, low-hanging vaulted ceilings, pilasters overdesigned for their bearing function, and apses and curved walls which Hoffmann imposed upon the preexisting geometry of the walls, thereby creating a magical and colorful effect not seen in his earlier work.

One of the side galleries

Entrance to the main gallery

Main room with Max Klinger's statue of Beethoven

1903   Pavilion for the
Wiener Werkstätte

Central gallery

Düsseldorf
"The pavilion as a mirror of the arts"

"Something always seemed to enwrap and secure the objects in space," wrote Rochowanski of Hoffmann's interiors. The arrangement of the Austrian pavilion at Düsseldorf is not as spatially complex as that of the Klinger room. However, the details and simple, linear elements reveal a refinement that will slowly come to constitute the very language of the Hoffmann style. The apparently casual arrangement of the objects without reference to their surroundings makes them appear permanently fixed in their spaces. The objects gaze at each other, alike and symmetrical as in a mirror: the two doors with their lozenge-shaped mullions, the pillars and marble busts in their niches.

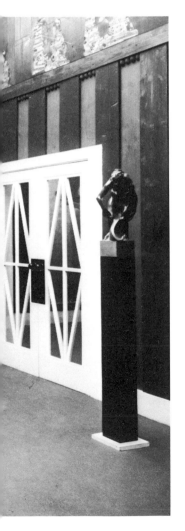

Niche with decorative vase

43

1904–1905 Interiors for the Wiener Werkstätte Exhibition

Vienna

Between 1902, the year of its founding, and 1905, when the first catalogue of the Wiener Werkstätte was published, Hoffmann prepared the first exhibition of Werkstätte objects for display in their own exhibition hall. In the empty, large space which on other occasions Hoffmann had not hesitated to fill with trees and gardens, the objects and exhibition structures confront each other, composing themselves into a whole where pilasters, niches, and apses lose their architectural substance and become imbued with an ephemeral existence that imparts its visual message to the very wall surfaces.

Each element—opaque and transparent planes, projections and recesses, floors and ceilings—is endowed with an autonomy, exhausting its own meanings without regard to its built surroundings.

Gallery with
Werkstätte *commode*

Wall with built-in cabinets

1904

"Little House"
Fashion Salon

Vienna

Only a year after its founding, the Wiener Werkstätte had begun to produce its own objects, including some pieces of furniture like those that appeared in the "Little House."

The salon which Hoffmann decorated and furnished in collaboration with Kolo Moser at Mariahilferstrasse 6 was one of the first examples of the master's novel technique of decoration: black and white lacquered elements conceived according to criteria that would become increasingly precise. Mirrored surfaces which heightened the reflectivity of the lacquered elements produced an unreal multiplication of spaces, creating an architecture of illusion, of non-existent spatiality. This is one of the most suggestive examples of an effect which Hoffmann would explore many times again. The constructional details are jewel-like in their precision.

Bureau with mirror

Corner of the "living room"

Corner of the showroom

Interior of the salon,
multiplied in the reflection
of the mirrors

1905–1906 Villa Beer-Hoffmann

Hasenauerstrasse 59, Vienna XVIII

The interiors of this house were completed at the same time as those of Dr. Wittgenstein's house, and contemporaneously with many drawings for the Palais Stoclet.

A resumption of the theme already worked out in the Spitzer house two years earlier, the Beer-Hoffmann house is a happy combination of interior decoration with architecture—an effect which Hoffmann unceasingly pursued. Here, every traditional distinction between furniture and surrounding space is overcome. The architectural space of the house is the result of a unity achieved between the detail work done by skilled craftsmen and the construction work of the builders. In Dr. Beer's large library, the supports of the bookcases continue along the walls to become part of the window wall. An "architectural will" pervades the entire house.

Library interior

Study

Entrance and stairs to the upper floor

The Construction of the Language

1904–1908   Purkersdorf Sanatorium

Vienna

Within the tradition of modern architecture, this work has been seen to anticipate rationalism, or to be an extreme imitation of Otto Wagner's work. On the contrary, it summarizes everything Hoffmann had achieved by this stage in his work: it is an object conceived on a grand scale, immersed in the woods that surround it, and joined to an existing pavilion by a covered, glazed loggia (which Hoffmann added later).

The almost disconcerting absoluteness of the plan derives from the rigid separation of the dining room from the living room and reading rooms by means of a corridor, which ends in the monumental "space" of a double-height hall. Every functional relationship on the horizontal plane is solved with the same logic as on the vertical, where the windows, lacking cornices and projections, open their transparent glass panes onto the facade. In contrast, the fragile, contradictory element of the top floor, a glazed penthouse that appears as a light crown, provokes a "floor by floor" reading of the building. Every detail of the building, including the interior decoration, was executed in Viennese workshops according to Hoffmann's and Moser's designs with an obsessive attention to detail, creating something more than simply a large therapeutic facility for a community of patients.

Although now altered, Purkersdorf still remains a complete integration of architectural structure, decoration, and furnishing—realizing the very program of the Wiener Werkstätte.

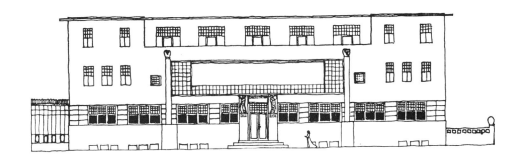

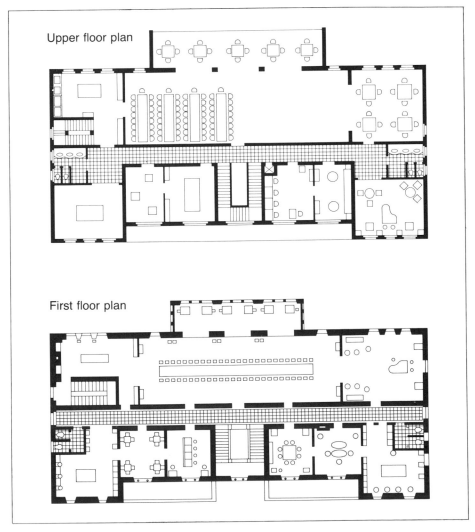

Upper floor plan

First floor plan

Perspective study of the facade

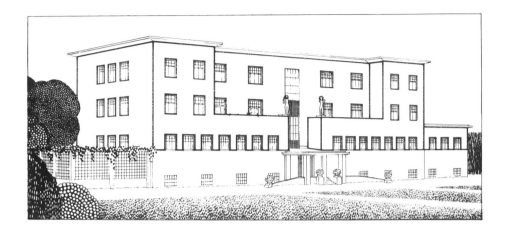

The rear facade today

Detail of the rear facade, facing the park, as it appears today

The glazed passageway
connecting the existing
pavilion

The main facade, at the time of construction

Detail of the rear canopy

The rear entrance

The front entrance

Dining room, with Wiener Werkstätte furniture

Entrance hall looking toward the stair (above)
and garden (below)

1905   Wittgenstein Apartment

Vienna

Among the many apartments decorated by Hoffmann between 1903 and 1905—from the celebrated interiors designed for Wärndorfer, the financial and administrative patron of the Werkstätte, to those for Biach, Fidgor, Brauner, and other influential figures associated with the Werkstätte—the Wittgenstein apartment in a certain sense concludes the early period of the style.

To a room planned by others, Hoffmann intervened once again by filling the space with his "ephemeral" but articulate architecture. The simple study, traditional in Viennese houses, was a sufficient pretext to create a domestic space which is, in fact, monumental, a fragment of the extensive formal vocabulary which he would use over and over again.

Interior of the study

Interior of the study

1905–1911   Palais Stoclet

275 Avenue de Tervueren, Brussels

Before Sekler described its development, the Palais Stoclet was one of the great enigmas of modern architecture. An exhaustive critical analysis of this most challenging of Hoffmann's buildings has yet to be done, although it has been variously described as "protorational", "decadent", and an embodiment of "the most vigorous ideals of the European bourgeoisie" (Persico). Its completion took the entire staff of the Wiener Werkstätte almost ten years, and Moser, Czeschka, Metzner, Minne, Klimt, Khnopff, and others worked there. Hoffmann's later investigations would take him along diverse paths, but all his previous work is summarized here, without the "absoluteness" of Purkersdorf.

The piano nobile of the building has a monumental hall, around which Hoffmann placed rooms of unusual dimensions: the bedroom, 9.50 × 5.70 meters, the bathroom, 6 × 6, the dining room with Klimt's famous mosaics, 15 × 7, and the music room, approximately 18 × 7.

The entire building—which was first proposed for the site on the Hohe Warte in Vienna where the Villa Ast later was built—is, notwithstanding its Turili (white Norwegian) marble bordered with worked bronze, less extravagant than many of Hoffmann's later works. His exceptional clients had allowed him complete freedom to work on the building as if it were a laboratory for the endless experiments of his studio and his collaborators. The rational naturalism of the architectural object thus was researched and emphasized from the exterior to the interior, in the decoration as well as in the garden, and the designer's rich historical imagination and experimental proclivity are evident in every detail.

The allusions to classicism, visible despite Hoffmann's conscious distortions, locks the building in an ordered and composed whole and places it in a world of lost archetypes: Roman, Flemish, Byzantine. In spite of its domestic forms the object is no longer recognizable in terms of type; located on the margins of a city largely composed of suburbs, more refined than anything most people are accustomed to, the Palais Stoclet, with its rarefied decorations and *objets d'art,* waits in its park for a silent crowd. Its sumptuous exterior, crowned by Metzner's sculptures, transforms it into an object with no other significance than an architectural one.

View on Avenue de Tervueren. From left to right, the covered passage of the main entrance, the stair tower volume with the crowning four statues of Hercules by Metzner, and the driveway with the suspended passerelle over the courtyard

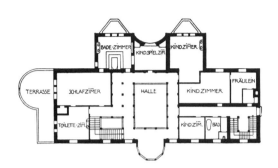

Second floor plan

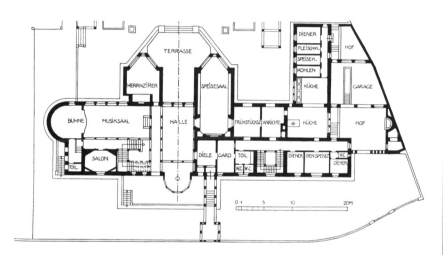

Ground floor plan

Basement floor plan

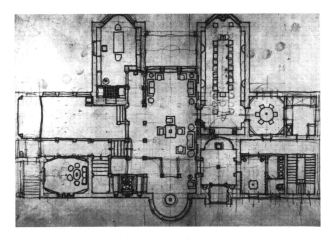

Preliminary plan of the
upper floor

Preliminary study of the ground floor plan

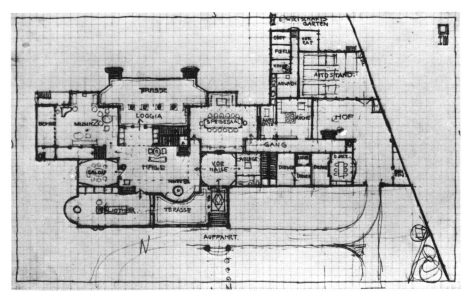

Ground floor plan.
Study drawing of the
final version

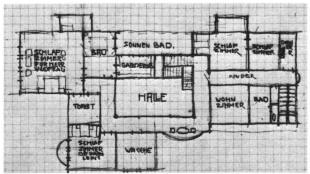

Rear elevation. Study drawing of the final version

Study of the rear facade facing the garden

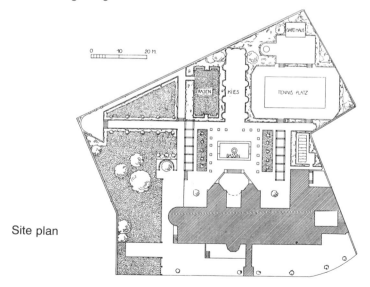

Site plan

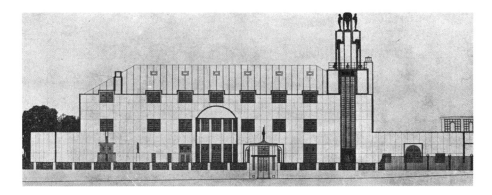

Front elevation

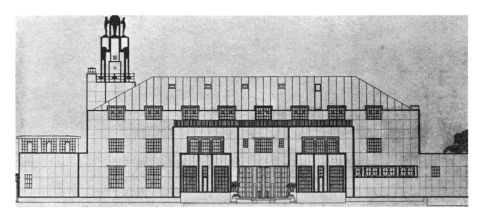

Rear elevation

Study of the rear facade
and garden. Watercolor,
ca. 1904

Model, 1905, seen from
the street side

Model, 1905, seen from the garden side

Driveway entrance and passerelle over the courtyard

Facade on Avenue de Tervueren, ca. 1931

View of the garden facade just after completion, seen from the swimming pool

One enters the vestibule between walls clad in antique green marble, embellished by Hoffmann with vases and gilded branches. The floor is of black and white paving stones, and the stucco ceiling with its straight gilt ridges is further decorated with a mosaic by Leopold Forstner.

The walls of the main hall are yellow-gold Italian marble, and the columns supporting the ceiling are of gray Belgian marble with black veining. Among the columns, Adolphe Stoclet's collection of Greek, Byzantine, and Roman sculpture was displayed on pedestals and in glass cases. Chinese and Japanese paintings and a large number of Italian primitives were hung on the walls. The entire floor was covered with a famous carpet designed by Hoffman himself, while heavy white Chinese silk hangings with ruches of yellow-brown silk created a magical atmosphere, inspiring the sense of wonderment spoken of by many who visited there at the time. In the music room, the chairs of the Werkstätte appeared in a gilded version, with purple upholstery, while the floor was inlaid with African paduk and teak in a double square grid pattern.

Balcony on the corner of the front facade

View of the main hall from the entrance

Interior of the music room. The walls, clad in marble from Portovenere, are outlined in gilded bronze. The organ, visible in the photograph, has now been removed.

Views from the vestibule and main hall toward the stair to the second floor

The master bedroom. All the furniture was made by the Werkstätte of blocks of inlaid rosewood.

Corridor in the service wing

Access from main hall to music room

Interior of the main hall looking toward the bay window and the upper gallery.
The concrete structure is clad in Italian Paonazzo marble, the furniture is by the
Wiener Werkstätte, and on the pedestals are Stoclet's collection of sculpture.

Gallery around the double-height hall, giving access to the bedrooms and the monumental bathroom

The fountain by Georg Minne in the apse of the main hall

The dining room, clad in marble from Portovenere. Note the refinement of the intarsia floor and the built-in furniture.

Entrance to the dining room

The dining room with its mosaics by Klimt, seen from the veranda

Interior of a children's playroom, decorated by Ludwig Jungnickel

Bedroom

The monumental
bathroom with black
marble floor, statuary
marble walls, and coral
pink furniture

The kitchen

The kitchen. The fixtures
are similar to those at
Purkersdorf

The covered veranda

View from the veranda towards the garden, on axis with the monumental fountain

View of the pergola in the garden

The fountain basin seen from the garages

The gazebo

The pergola

In Hoffmann's plan, the axis of the "water obelisk" in the fountain basin cuts through the terrace and covered veranda, intersecting the small fountain in the main hall, and terminating in the apse facing Avenue de Tervueren.

1906–1907 Villa Hochstätter

Steinfeldgasse, Vienna

During the construction of the Palais Stoclet and before he became engrossed in the important new commission for the Villa Ast, Hoffmann was involved in building two villas in Vienna: the Beer-Hoffmann and the Hochstätter, the latter radically altered today. In 1906 the Wittgenstein family also commissioned him to design their country house, in which one may see his earlier style further mellowed by the language of the Werkstätte.

The Villa Hochstätter on Steinfeldgasse is especially significant in this regard, for it is a further simplification of the concept of the house, brought to an almost brutal compression of the object into itself. The house does not communicate with its surroundings except by allusion (as will be true of the Villa Ast), and its elements are miniaturized almost to the point of caricature, creating a composition of altogether different scale.

Here, Fräulein Hochstätter had her small "palace" with a porticoed atrium, a Flemish-Pompeian garden, and, within the limits of economy, rich and refined detail on both the interior and exterior. Majolica substitutes for marble, masonry is faced with brick, but the intention is the same: the house is forever linked to those who built it, to the extent of becoming hostile to any "other" person who might later inhabit it. This may be seen in the discordant quality of the later interior renovations.

View along Steinfeldgasse

The kitchen, with fixtures designed by Hoffmann

1906–1907 Country House for the Wittgenstein Family

Hohenberg, Austria

This is one of Hoffmann's less well known works, planned at the same time as the Villa Hochstätter and the Beer-Hoffmann house. Contemporary photographs of the yard and interior show Hoffmann's attempt to conform to the local vernacular style, creating a typically indigenous dwelling. The facade is coldly punctuated with fenestration and hardly enriched by the elongated window of the living room. The entrance, crowned with a *Goldendach*, still seems to echo Olbrich.

Entrance

The stair

The house in the last stages of construction

1907

Interior of the Cabaret Fledermaus

Vienna

The concept of a place where the Viennese avant-garde could meet at night and which could, at the same time, be shown to foreign visitors as an example of the work of the Wiener Werkstätte was proposed by the financier Wärndorfer. Here, Rochowanski recalled, Hoffmann created such vivacious colors and decorative details that the cabaret became the very symbol of the period and its style. Peter Altenberg's poetry was read there, Beardsley recited verses, and Mela Mars, dressed in a costume designed by Hoffmann (who in those years loved to design clothing for the *femmes fatales* of Vienna), sung Goethe's *Bekehrte*. It was a favorite meeting place, and Klimt, Ewers, and Emil Orlik could frequently be seen there.

The entire design, with all its furniture, was later manufactured for the famous Kohn collection.

1908   Kunstschau

Vienna

In 1908 the Werkstätte group was given the opportunity to build a new pavilion for temporary exhibitions—the Kunstschau. Hoffmann, Moser, Kokoshka, Schiele, and Gütersloh collaborated on this with Klimt, who seems to have been the initiator. The building, constructed on the Lothringerstrasse, site of the future Konzerthaus, was for a long time considered the prototype of the tendency later seen in the design for the Austrian pavilion in Rome.

The massive concrete walls, contrasting with the fragile, tattoo-like surface decoration and the rigorous plan suggesting a return to classicism, indicate Hoffmann's definite desire to combat the avant-garde on the very iconographic grounds from which he himself was excluded. The building was inaugurated with an exhibition of furniture executed for the Palais Stoclet and pictorial works by members of the group.

Axonometric drawing

View of the main entrance

The Memory of Classicism

1909–1911   Villa Ast on the Hohe Warte

Steinfeldgasse 2, Vienna XIX

Situated on the brow of the hill overlooking Kahlenberg and the Vienna Woods, the Villa Ast, with its surprising and "strange" presence, completes the famous residential colony. The house is constructed of reinforced concrete, decorated and incised as if it were marble, and raised above the ground plane on a base of rough quarried stone. A wall enclosure makes the interior inaccessible to view from the outside.

In contrast to the complex exterior design, the planimetric distribution of space on the interior is based on a very natural functionalism. The house projects towards the garden in a knowing game of conforming to and overcoming the grade changes in the natural and built levels. The refinement of the interiors—today badly remodeled—was perhaps even more *recherché* than that of the Palais Stoclet because of Ast's and Hoffmann's unusual decision to organize it around Klimt's two famous paintings: the *Danae* and *The Sisters*.

The Villa Ast has only recently been discovered by modern critics; it was kept secret from the history of architecture for a long time in spite of Levetus' celebration of it in *Moderne Bauformen* in 1913 at the height of modernist polemical fervor. It is without doubt Hoffmann's most consistent achievement after the Palais Stoclet. It clearly manifests his interest in taking the classical language in the direction indicated by Riegl, while at the same time subverting the rules in an intense game that has no peers and precludes all possibility of imitation.

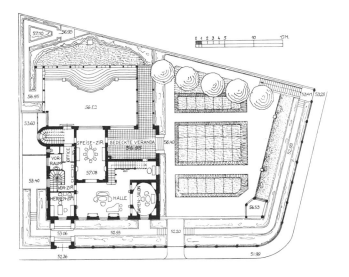

Site plan at the level of
the main hall, with the
garden and "simulated
swimming pool" of
grass and water

The villa seen from the garden of the Spitzer house

Rear facade looking toward the swimming pool

The entrance to the upper-level garden terrace. Note the refinement of the giant-order pilasters of the facade.

View from the main hall

Stair to the garden on the upper level

91

Corner of the living room

Stair in the main hall to upper level

The dining room, looking toward the main hall

Study

Detail of the dining room, with window on the garden at rear

Corridor of the upper floor, with balcony balustrade of carved
wood, lacquered white

The covered veranda, with the entrance to the dining room

The kitchen, with the
white lacquered
furniture of the
Werkstätte

1910   Second Moll House

Wollergasse 10, Vienna XIX

Constructed after the Villa Ast and before the completion of the Villa Primavesi, the second Moll House in Vienna, also on the Hohe Warte, was the last decisive attempt by Hoffmann at a "simplication" of the style. The facade of the house is reduced to a single sign, symbol of the house itself, almost aggressive in the naive linearity of its cubic and spired space—an exaltation of "ordinariness."

    The entire construction, quite modest in its dimensions, is then further refined by the repetitive use of simple Greek decorative motifs, already used on a number of other occasions, as in the design for the villa on the Hohe Warte which was published in *Der Architekt,* no. 16.

Facade on Wollergasse

Detail of the front door

Details of the small balcony on the upper floor

1910 Project for a Small Theater in Kapfenberg

Main facade on the piazza

Styria, Austria

This work was almost contemporary with the Austrian Pavilion in Rome. Hoffmann, who had worked for more than a year on the project for the Ast family, used figurative elements similar to those in the Palais Stoclet. The solidity of the theater, which was to have completed a block of buildings, is counterpointed by the figurative and almost mannered lightness of the surface decoration. This large, box-like structure, another product of the workshops of the Wiener Werkstätte, did not lack unique detailing: the "negative" corners accentuate by their absence the convexity of the facade, which projects onto the outer surface the delicate interior decoration. There is no relationship between the building and its setting, however. As Hoffmann would say later, the city is a totality in the process of perpetual, timeless formation, immobilized like the figures gazing at each other in the piazza.

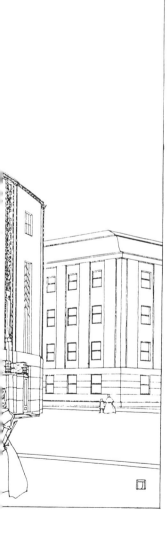

Interior

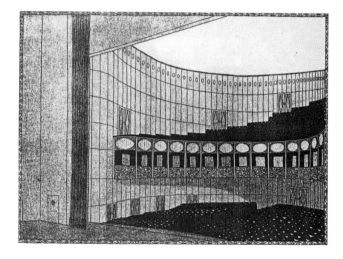

1911 Austrian Pavilion at the Rome Exhibition

The fiftieth anniversary of the founding of the Kingdom of Italy was celebrated with a major exhibition in Rome which attracted architects from all over Europe. The Austrians were represented by the Secession and by Hoffmann's large pavilion which, while not ignoring the ceremonial aspects of the exhibition, interpreted and transformed them, subtly making them subordinate to his other concerns.

A series of fluted perimeter columns, embedded in the walls on the sides and becoming free-standing towards the interior of the squared courtyard, supports a large roof that appears to have no cornice or ceiling weight to carry and also is deeply fluted; this makes the pilasters seem to continue beyond the vertical wall plane in a horizontal direction. Two apses face each other on either side of the central assembly room, with Klimt's allegory *Justice* exhibited in the semicircular apse.

Inspired perhaps by the local context, Hoffmann made his building respond to the natural implications of the site: the structure is suffused by a mythic atmosphere, and it appears monumental more by virtue of its allusions than its actual forms. Certainly the fundamental concept is that of a temple; nevertheless the work remains within the established tradition of the master. It is human in scale, the product of manual and intellectual labor, demanding its own celebration, subtly rhetorical perhaps, but rich in a freedom of language found elsewhere only in the later work of Le Corbusier.

The language of Vienna was elitist, and it required silent contemplation. As eloquently represented in the work of Klimt, Vienna was a "culture of mosaics."

Preliminary plan

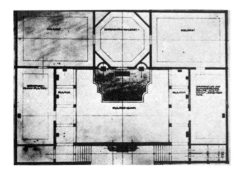

Final plan

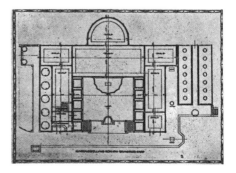

Rendering of the facade, looking towards the terraces of the Valley Giulia

Elevation

Entrance portico, looking from the right side of the building towards the steps on the left side

1912–1914 Colony of Villas in Kaasgraben

Kaasgrabengasse 30–38 and Suttingergasse 12–18, Vienna XIX

This group of six houses was built for friends or acquaintances of the Wiener Werkstätte, some of them painters and portrait photographers. Therefore, many of the houses have a studio with large windows. Hoffmann experimented here with decorative motifs current in domestic vernacular architecture, using stenciling on the interior walls and horizontal ribbing on the heavy concrete cornices. The loggias and balconies face the gardens in the back. Dr. Vetter, one of the clients and a personal friend of Hoffmann's, later wrote to him: "My house is so beautiful, so precious, so clear, that living there constantly fills us with joy. . . . It is of small dimensions, but to us it seems as enormous as a palace, amplified everywhere by the artistic skills which created it. At times I stop in front of a window, and the enjoyment I experience from its noble, pure proportions is far greater than anything I could experience in a gallery of paintings. . . . It is an immense privilege to receive this work from you—not to own it, because it will always belong to you and to our period, but to be its custodians. We are highly honored to carry out such a responsibility."

Here, Hoffmann truly worked magic, responding totally to functional requirements, but translating them into forms more complex and subtle than Dr. Vetter could ever have thought of.

View of the first two houses in the last stages of completion

Detail of the roof

Service entrance

Kaasgrabengasse 32–34, facade

Details of the facade

Suttingergasse 12–14, garden facade

Detail of the facade

Garden window

1913–1915 Villa Primavesi

Gloriettegasse 14–16, Vienna XIII

About the time Wärndorfer took over the administration of the Wiener Werkstätte, Otto Primavesi, a leading financier in Vienna, decided to build a villa for entertainment purposes in the Gloriettegasse, a small street on the edge of Schönbrunn Park. Hoffmann was asked to design a "custom-made" residence as challenging in scope as the Villa Ast or the Palais Stoclet, including every detail of the decoration and the interior furnishings: a handmade masterpiece. Several members of the Wiener Werkstätte also were associated in its design. The villa was to be situated in a spacious park; subsequently this was transformed into a garden.

Even though the interiors are not as sumptuous as those of Hoffmann's other patrician residences, the exterior, especially the facade on Gloriettegasse, is more spectacular than anything he had previously produced. The two side volumes of the building, with tympanums displaying allegorical works by Anton Hanak, lock the sequence of pilasters and wall in a sinuous progression. Projecting from the pilasters in place of the abacus are small brackets holding female statues. The effect of the juxtaposition of the two fixed and pedimented side planes with the curvilinear sequence of pilasters in the central area of the facade, heightened by radiant light and sharp shadows, is to give the building an immeasurable spatiality.

Entrance portico on
Gloriettegasse

Although the building possesses a jewel-like perfectionism, to be appreciated at a close distance, it is in fact better experienced when seen from afar, for a closer view obscures its architectural unity. Only one early photograph of the facade survives among the archival documents; however, the sensation one still has when approaching the villa today is certainly that of an object scaled to the eye of the viewer. The transverse section runs from the 5- to 6-meter facade on Gloriettegasse to the double-height facade facing the garden. Hidden by a wall from the view of passers-by, it is treated in a manner that is exacting if, paradoxically, full of secrets. If we compare the decorative details here with those of the Villa Ast, it seems as if the whole building is in relief; the coloration is more intense, warmed by an antique gold impasto, and the grooves in the pilasters are softer, almost canonical in their proportions.

Plan of the piano nobile

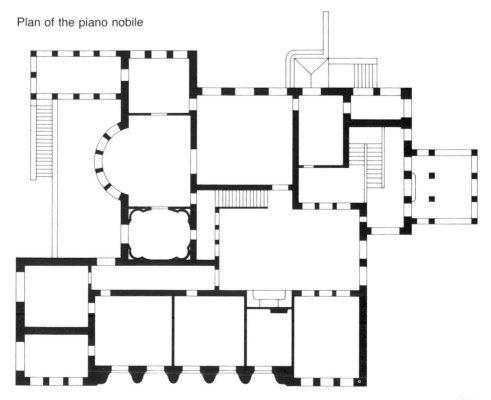

Floral decoration in between the pilasters, side elevation

Statue on a pilaster on the front elevation

Facade facing Gloriettegasse

Tympanum with Anton Hanak's sculpture

Facade on Gloriettegasse,
with entrance gate at
second-floor level

Rear facade today, after recent restorations

Detail of the west facade

Detail of the rear facade

112

West facade

West facade:
the apsidal volume

113

A more tranquil Viennese refinement emerges in the interiors, decorated with marble and both carved and plain wood, endowing the building with the quality of empty space, of a void that paradoxically is positive, "designed."

In the rear, the entire house has double-height windows overlooking a fanciful garden—today largely compromised by strange arboreal elements and added terraces—where pools of water, fountains, little bridges, and gazebos are ordered in a precise and compressed space, expanded by perspectival effects such as the unusual device of using outdoor mirrors on the gazebo walls. Seated in the shade of the roof of a little Greek temple, in the small space of two square meters, one may look at one's own shadow reflected in the lead-white surfaces, as well as at the soft vastness of the Vienna sky and the variety of the botanical world in the surrounding garden.

Double-height entrance

Stairway leading to upper floor

Detail of the window in the main hall

Main hall with wood intaglio decoration as it appears today

Detail

Main hall in a photograph of the period

Dining room. Note the bands of marble used to define edges

The gazebo seen from the wall surrounding the site

The greenhouse, now destroyed

The motif on the white lacquered wood fence echoes the one in bronze on the exterior gate.

Detail of the gazebo, showing one of the mirrored bays

The gazebo, the fountain, and the white lacquered wood fence

The gazebo as it was in 1913

1914 Austrian Pavilion at the German Werkbund Exhibition

Cologne, Germany

Hoffmann collaborated with several artists of the Wiener Werkstätte—among them Oskar Strnad, Dagobert Peche, Eduard Wimmer, and Fritz Novotny—on the pavilion for this exhibition in Cologne, and with them adopted an unusual solution to the "metaphysics" of the interior rooms. These were contained by the large open-air pavilion where every single national group in the Hapsburg empire was to display its products.

In spite of the austerity of its exterior, which it would be an oversimplification to attribute only to Hoffmann's neoclassical tendencies, the entire pavilion is really a "magic box." It is apparently solid but one can perceive its ephemeral, precarious existence; above all it communicates the temporary quality of an enormous cardboard carton. The two pediments, as heavy as the inscriptions upon them and set back from the facade plane (thereby violating every architectural rule), float above a transparent space rhythmically divided by pilasters. These call to mind other spaces and architectural forms which lie between the improvisatory and the celebratory, an architecture of veils, mirrors, and inlaid surfaces such as one sees in a magic theater. It also has a source in Pompeian geometry. This is the height of the art of illusion.

Facade facing the *Festhalle*

Hoffmann's "drawing room"

Facade facing the *Festhalle*, showing the central courtyard open to the sky

1914

Pavilion for the Leipzig Publishing Exhibition

Leipzig, Germany

Although often overlooked, the Leipzig pavilion in fact reveals a new way of working for Hoffmann. Inscriptions praising work and extolling the civic role of printing and publishing, arches in a style somewhere between Arabic and Art Déco, and above all an excessive use of decorative elements along the edges of spatial dividers characterize the pavilion. The aphoristic words on the portal have a synthetic function: to "explain" the significance of things, while the black and white color scheme of the Werkstätte seems to imply, "whatever the style, Moorish or something else, it all has to do with Vienna."

Pavilion interiors

1914

Country House for the Primavesi Family

Winkelsdorf, Moravia

Completely destroyed by fire only a few years after its completion, this second Primavesi house was famous for its unique use of the vernacular together with a modern architectural vocabulary.

Hoffmann in fact juxtaposed with a concrete structure columns in the form of tree trunks barely stripped of bark, and other elements of a rustic flavor. The ground level, faced in rough red stone, was likewise juxtaposed with an apse having refined decoration and materials. The entire building was covered with a thatched roof in the typical shape of a low arch.

At the time of its destruction, the house contained Otto Primavesi's celebrated collection of paintings, antiques, and manuscripts as well as all the furniture specifically designed by Hoffmann for the house.

Front elevation

Side elevation

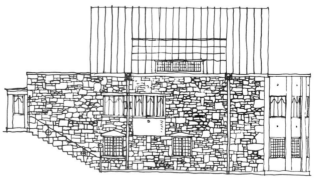

1917

Project for a Palace of Culture and Thought

Stockholm

The idea of a temple-like building dedicated to European culture and thought was discussed over and over again during these years in Paris and Berlin as well as in Stockholm, finally to be concluded in Geneva with the Mundaneum of Le Corbusier and Paul Otlet. Hoffmann's project, which had a facade of 150 meters and contained exhibition halls celebrating the fruits of both intellectual and manual labor, was organized around a large central auditorium for performances and concerts. The modular construction, supporting three pyramids and two obelisk-like antennae, repeats themes previously used in the pavilions in Cologne and Rome.

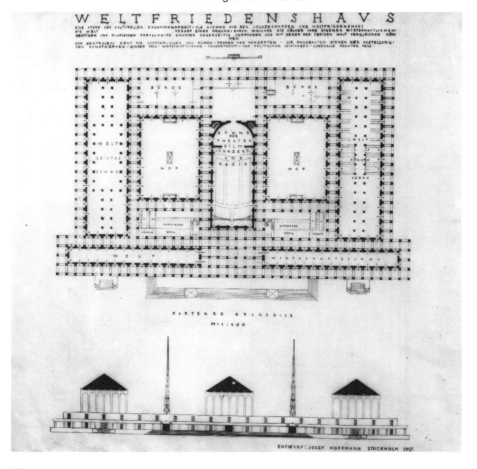

1923

Ast Country House on the Wörthersee

Velden, Carinzia

The five years between 1920 and 1925 were years of crisis and transition for Hoffmann. The search which had occupied him began to proceed along different lines from the course which would conclude in the design for the house of Sonia Knips, and it already showed signs of being affected by the international language of the European avant-garde. The Ast Country House in Velden is the classic product of a thinly disguised curiosity which would later develop into a more irreverent interest in these international developments.

On a solitary site on a thickly wooded hill of larch trees sloping down to the lake, Hoffmann organized a sequence of grassy terraces connected by ramps. The building is visible from the lake as a series of successive planes, the strongly accentuated perspective defined by sharp, horizontal cornices without any logical conclusion or crown. The box-like house, provisory shelter for a life within a vast woods, and containing a charming garden equipped with gazebos and pergolas of roses, then turns in on itself. The small windows and portholes open almost casually in the walls.

On the opposite side of the house from the main entrance, a porthole surmounted by a loggia decorated with a frieze by Anton Hanak marks the end of the ramped path to the house. The interiors still show the signs of this memorable epoch. Hansel and Gretel's house has been succeeded by a new conception.

The upper floor and the pitched roof were added later.

The house in 1923

The house with its land-
scaped terracing, seen
from the pergola by the
lake

Pergola in the garden

The house as it appears
today, seen from the lake

Detail of the frieze of bacchantic dancers by Anton Hanak underneath the loggia

Entrance hall

The portal and loggia on the facade facing the lake

1923–1924   Knips House

Front facade seen from the lawn of the neighboring house

Nusswaldgasse 20, Vienna XIX

This is the last in the series of famous Viennese villas. Hoffmann had at this time completed the Ast Country House in Velden, the Villa Dunkel in Budapest, his own apartment in the Schleifmühlgasse, and the Sigmund-Berl house in Freudenthal, and he had begun work for the new socialist government in Austria.

For Sonia Knips, he reduced the house to its most drastic typological simplification, limiting to a minimum the number of interior walls and replacing them with glass partitions. Unlike the Villa Primavesi, this house in set back from the street, with enough lawn to allow a comprehensive and strictly frontal view of its facade. The otherwise symmetrical facade, which is entirely faced in slate and has small lozenges projecting from its dark shadows, like those on the protruding dadoes of the west wall of the temple of Athena Nike, is asymmetricized by the off-center placement of the door. Within this composition of rigorous architectural rhythms, the file of windows in their projecting frames conveys a sense of the empty space of rooms where once "every available surface was occupied by Klimt's paintings."

The edges of the interior volumes, which in the Villa Primavesi were marked on the exterior by an inflected cornice line, here are emphasized by an indentation, thus inverting the natural conclusion of the geometry. For Hoffmann a house was now simply four walls defining an area on the ground. From this point on, any effort to articulate "differences" would be meaningless to him: here, the facade facing the large, fantastical garden—once framed by a wall over which an ancient walnut tree cast a deep shadow—would be identical to the front facade were it not for the projection of a portion of the ground floor and terrace above.

First floor window

The intersection of the
front and side facades

Sonia Knips' boudoir

The villa seen from the garden in a photograph of 1925

Glass-fronted cupboards in the kitchen

Library

Study in the attic

Bedroom

The Celebration of Social Democracy

1924   Klosehof

Philippovichgasse 1, Vienna XIX

This apartment block designed by Hoffmann is surprising in the heterogeneous iconographic context of socialist Vienna, with its mixture of Gothic, German Expressionist, late-Cubist, and Wagnerian elements. It also is innovative in terms of its declared intention to bring into this new political climate the results of architectural explorations which had previously had an entirely different clientele (Gessner, Schopper, Kalesa, Theiss).

Today this work still appears out of place in Vienna. Built of dark gray, rough material in a volumetric geometry punctuated by the dark, deep recesses of balconies and by minimally articulated stairwells crowned by rounded tympanums, the block is four stories high with 140 apartments of 50 to 60 square meters each.

Facade on
Werkmanngasse

Ground floor plan

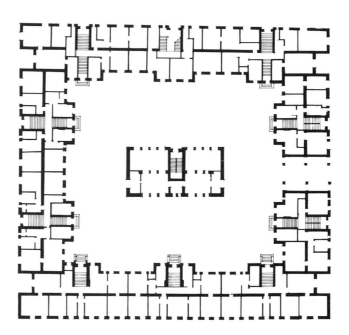

Front and back elevations
of the central tower block

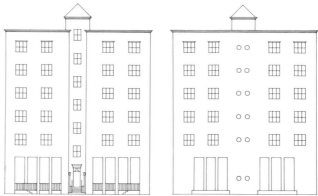

Philippovichgasse elevation

Courtyard

Entrance hall on the
Werkmanngasse side

Entrance to the tower block

The tower block in the courtyard

A large, monumental entranceway with pilasters allows access to the courtyard, from which one enters the different interior elevations. In the center of the courtyard stands a tall building which contains more apartments, a gymnasium, and service spaces. Compared with Hoffmann's earlier structures, Klosehof is not afraid of proclaiming its monumentality in a closed world that denies its surroundings. Through its portals crowned with statues symbolizing work and liberty, one arrives in a world and a time that proudly reveal their own "difference." This is an urban building which cannot but cause the modernists to acknowledge a sense of loss; its archetype, betrayed by the avant-garde, has by this time faded into an uneasy remoteness.

Facade on Philippovichgasse

Detail showing lighting of street number

Detail of a balustrade

Commemorative plaque

Entrance to the courtyard from
Philippovichgasse

Entrance to a stairwell off the courtyard

1924 Winarskyhof

Stromstrasse 36–38, Vienna XX

Entrance from
Stromstrasse

This is a more challenging block. It was built for the socialist administration at the end of 1924, and covers the area in the XXth *Bezirk* that runs from Stromstrasse to Kaiserwasserstrasse. The entire block is then cut by Leystrasse. Hoffmann was given the strip facing Stromstrasse; Strnad, Josef Frank, and Oskar Wlach were given the other edges of the site; and Peter Behrens, who in 1922 took charge of classes at the Academy in Vienna, designed the main block. It was, in fact, a block within a block.

While Behrens produced a design of exceptional iconographic vigor, decorating the walls with symbols and fragments, Hoffmann, in contrast to his own previous work, including the Klosehof, chose a more tranquil style adapted from the vernacular tradition: white plaster wall surfaces, a plinth in gray concrete, and tympanums reduced to a timid accent on top of the stair towers. Leystrasse flows through the facade of the building, passes through the tense portals of Behrens and Strnad, and terminates beyond the last set of arches in the broad space of the street on the other side of the complex. Hoffmann responded to the disconcerting severity of Behren's work by drawing upon the very roots of his own culture. Whether socialist or bourgeois, elitist or populist, Vienna spoke first and foremost of *Heimatkunst*.

General site plan
with Hoffmann's building
in black

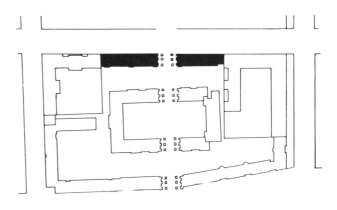

Floor plan

Rear facade

A Defense of the Ephemeral

1924–1925 From the Wiener Werkstätte to the Style of the Twentieth Century

1928 marked the 25th anniversary of the founding of the Wiener Werkstätte, and for this occasion Hoffmann himself drew up a balance sheet. Only three years earlier, when Paul Poiret still was the high priest of Art Déco and the grand celebration took place on the Esplanade des Invalides in Paris, the end of the decorative arts movement was already in sight. In Vienna, the Werkstätte continued its production in a dignified and detached manner; its products were marketed in the United States, Switzerland, Italy, and Germany, where the aristocratic Viennese style provided an antidote to proletarian rationalism.

But is this facile distinction historically accurate? After fifty years and with a better understanding of the work of the Viennese, it is possible to see that Persico was somewhat hasty in his judgment: "... the cars stopped in Kärntnerstrasse [for the dissolution of the Wiener Werkstätte] meant not that Hoffmann was an artist without clients . . . but that the Palais Stoclet in Brussels, the Graben Cafe, and the hundred other things he had created . . . most typified an outmoded style, that of the Secession, and most represented a certain class, the bourgeoisie, which by that time was beginning to decline even in Austria."

It is a fact that an "architect of the Viennese bourgeoisie" had at that time only two possibilities: either to join the international movement and thereby survive both economically and otherwise, or to push the game to its very limits, towards the extremes of a reactionary language, overrefined to the point of becoming nothing but a monologue. One man undertook this subtle game— Hoffmann's pupil Dagobert Peche, whose countless furniture designs and interiors show evidence of Hoffmann's style even further wrought The shock which one still experiences today when confronted with the works of these two designers during these years arises from an overriding belief that an emphasis on detail clearly opposes the "purification" of taste. Yet at the same time the detail is the essence of the work, a part of the whole, embodying the very significance of civilization.

Viennese interiors by Hoffmann, 1924

Interiors with Wiener Werkstätte furniture, 1927

Library with small marble fireplace, Vienna, 1930

Desk designed by Dagobert Peche and executed by the Wiener Werkstätte, ca. 1920

Interior of a restaurant, Vienna, 1930

Living room, Vienna, 1930

1925

Austrian Pavilion at the International Exhibition of Decorative Arts

Paris

For this event, Hoffmann coordinated the group of Austrians, including Strnad, who was commissioned to do the famous organ tower; Behrens, who produced the glass greenhouse; and Frank, who, with Hoffmann, designed the well-known furniture for the Café Viennois. The large pavilion, which covered more than one thousand square meters, was located between the Cours de la Reine and the bank of the Seine. Hoffmann joined the two parts with a colonnaded building which connected the boulevard to a terrace on the Seine. According to the official catalogue of 1925, it was a " . . . fantastic labyrinth of galleries and corridors onto which small rooms and niches opened, giving one the impression of being on a picturesque voyage, full of surprises." The "complexity" and atmosphere full of fantasy noted by all who saw Hoffmann's pavilion are even evident today in the photographs of the period. Above a solid concrete base, three horizontal fascias, separated by slightly projecting cornice lines, mark the entire extent of the building. Here and there on the exterior surfaces are inscriptions in relief with names of composers, artists, and works of art. In 1925, the critics spoke of Hoffmann's impromptu "conversion to the Italian baroque." In fact, the master of Pirnitz was using many of his previous themes, but as is typical of his work in the years preceding his experiments with functionalism, tending to push the style to extremes. Behind a metal cage with mirrored and glazed walls and surfaces was displayed a comprehensive exhibition of the Wiener Werkstätte, with some portions dedicated to Austrian craftsmanship. Black and white as well as floral decorations led to the room containing sculptures, culminating with Anton Hanak's *Flamme humaine.*

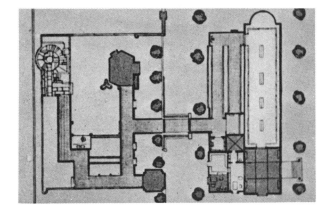

Schematic plan of the
final design of the pavilion

Photograph of the wood
model, 1924

Exterior of the central room dedicated to the Wiener Werkstätte

Entrance

The movable bureau, designed by
Hoffman for the exhibition

Connection between the two building wings

Entrance

Detail of the portico

Mirrored room displaying the products of the Wiener Werkstätte

1928–1929 Project for a Palace of the Arts on the Karlsplatz

Perspective study

Photomontage with the new palace inserted into the site on the Karlsplatz

Vienna

There had been a series of proposals by architects, including Hasenauer, Wagner, and Olbrich, for the intellectual center of Vienna, the Karlsplatz. Hoffmann's project for a palace of the arts, which also contains a conference and convention hall, shows his interest at this time in works on an urban scale. His proposals for the redevelopment of the Stadtpark and the Wienermesse are also from this period.

This building of steel and glass, with its Miesian echoes and resemblance to a contemporaneous project for a sanatorium at Salzburg, is a radical simplification of earlier works, an almost unexpected return to the style of Purkersdorf and the Palais Stoclet. On top of a base of square stones, rhythmically punctuated by window openings, rises a metal-cage structure, decisively accented on the horizontal and covered with a traditional pitched roof which contrasts with the prism of the tall tower block. The entire building was to have been traversed by an underpass which would have cut through the base and reduced the section of the overhanging block to only one floor, with the effect of levitating the upper volume above the base of anchoring piers. For Hoffmann, as for Wagner, Vienna was a city perpetually in the process of completion.

Perspective view of the model looking toward the tower block

1929

Showroom for the Wiener Werkstätte

Vienna

This is one of the many showrooms designed for the Wiener Werkstätte between 1925 and 1930, when the demand for their products was at its greatest.

The idea of a mirrored "box" was still in the air. The element of the portal, on a scale similar to that of the Ast Country House at Velden, is made less dominant by the addition of the simple sign on the glazed facade. This sign, which serves a decorative function, is an idea which Hoffmann frequently used in his work for the Werkstätte in this period. One may alse see his childish delight in repeating the motif of the red and white flag of the Republic on the pediment of the portal.

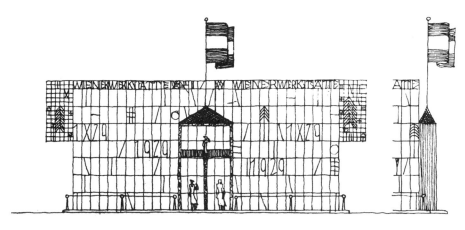

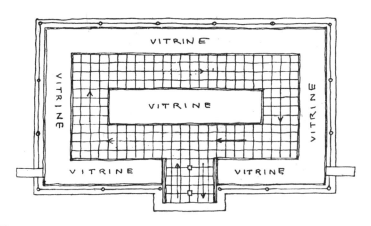

Details of the shop as it was built

1930

Austrian Pavilion at the German Werkbund Exhibition

Vienna

After the exhibition organized by the German Werkbund at the Weissenhofsiedlung in Stuttgart, where Josef Frank's proposal met with considerable interest, Hoffmann and Frank together assumed the vice-presidency of the Austrian division of the Werkbund in 1930.

The exhibition they organized that year in Vienna formed part of the celebrations in conjunction with the Werkbund Congress. Different events were staged in various parts of the city, and Frank, Strnad, and Walter Sobotka collaborated with Hoffmann to create many of the displays, including the famous Terrace Café. Hoffmann, however, designed the entire main exhibition hall himself, conceiving it as a trapezoidal space filled with light and color, with an allegorical monument to the arts in its center.

For the terrace and garden of the café, Hoffmann once again used the pergola motif employed in the Ast and Primavesi villas. Contemporary journals attest to Hoffmann's successful return here to the domain of the "ephemeral" after his difficult experience with residential blocks.

Study by Josef Frank for the cafe and concert room at the exhibition

Study by Hoffmann for the main exhibition hall

Cafe

Interior of the main hall

The Wind of Rationalism

1928

Prototype for a Prefabricated Steel House

In 1928, the firm of Vogel & Nott asked Hoffmann to design a prefabricated house of corrugated sheet metal, using a system similar to that employed for temporary railroad installations. This project came out of the general climate of experimentation in low-cost housing by many large European industries at this time. After the experiences in Vienna and Frankfurt, it had become increasingly evident that the responsibility for solving the problematic housing issue should be transferred to the public sector.

Private industry reacted typically with a strong interest in defining and standardizing elements, and in finding production systems which would incorporate prefabrication and a design process with built-in criteria of maximum economy.

The production costs which Mart Stam had sought to reduce through clarification and revision of the building typology already in use could, on the contrary, only be brought down by sharply cutting back on surface area, bringing the dwelling to its *Existenzminimum*, and owning up to the idea of the house as an assembly line product. The house proposed by Hoffmann (never produced) had an area of over 100 square meters and was not dissimilar in plan from contemporary houses in the international functionalist style.

The building, to be put together on site, sits on a base of light brick or stone aggregate. The main entrance is enclosed in a white pergola—a kind of atrium between the house and the city.

1928–1929 Building for the Sarmej Company

Cluj, Hungary

Although completely altered today, the Sarmej building, like other works of this period, shows Hoffmann's attempt to incorporate the elements of functionalism into his own style. The ribbon window is only "suggested" by a cut in the wall plane, but it still has a traditional quality about it. Similarly, the doorway, which is only an entry to the workshop, retains its function as a passage without losing its significance as a noble architectural element. The window frames, curiously set back from the facade plane—an unusual device for Hoffmann—allow the cornices to project strong shadows onto the glass plane, creating plastic effects on the wall similar to those in certain of his works of the first decade of the century.

1930

Project for a Housing Complex

Vienna XIX

Among the projects which accompanied the festivities celebrating the Werkbund Congress of 1930, Hoffmann was commissioned to design a housing complex in the XIXth *Bezirk* of Vienna.

His proposal incorporates three building types used in analogous projects: a *Miethaus* block with a vaguely Miesian flavor (a reference to the building in Stuttgart as well as to other projects), a three-story multi-family house, and stepped-back, terraced housing that was especially popular with the local residents. Especially in the third type it is fully evident that Hoffmann had by now accepted the vocabulary of the International Style without further reservations. The building contains all the elements of the most orthodox functionalism: the flat roof, the living room opening onto a wide terrace, the sleeping area overlooking the rear garden, the garage with access from the street.

But the round portholes, which no one had ever dared to use except for stairwells or service areas, here become architectural elements ordering the entire facade, abstract enough to free themselves from "the style."

The multi-family house: facade facing the street

The *Miethaus* block: street facade

The terraced housing: street facade

The terraced housing: garden facade

1928–1929 Project for a Sanatorium

Salzburg

The Bauhaus language of functionalist elements which emerges in Hoffmann's project for a sanatorium in Salzburg represents an unusual interlude in Hoffmann's work between 1928 and 1929. Already in the next year, in his project for the XIXth *Bezirk*, Hoffmann would demonstrate his preference for the International Style, which he considered to have a greater chance of overcoming the rigid code of rationalism. Here, he affirms the complete extraneousness of any decorative or symbolic form to the hospital's function. The concept is completely abstract, like the gridded lunar landscape from which it emerges in the rendering.

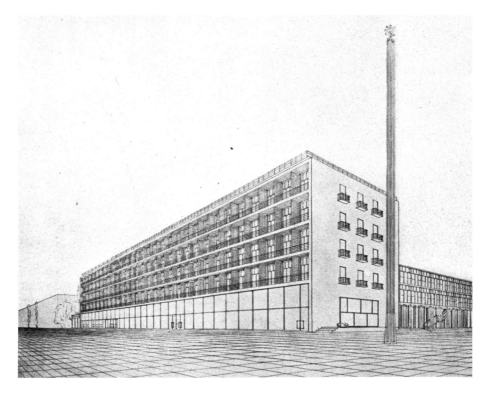

1932   Row Housing for the Werkbundsiedlung

Veitingergasse 79–83, Vienna XIII

The proposal to construct a group of high-, medium-, and low-rise housing blocks, as contemplated in the debates of CIAM as well as internationally, had been the object of a program propounded by Josef Frank in the general context of building activity in Vienna. The authorities subsequently reduced the scope of the program, stipulating low-rise housing as the only type to be built. A site was given on the edge of the city in an area previously considered unbuildable, and the use of the traditional colors—white, ochre, and dark red—was prescribed.

Aerial view of the *Siedlung* just after construction

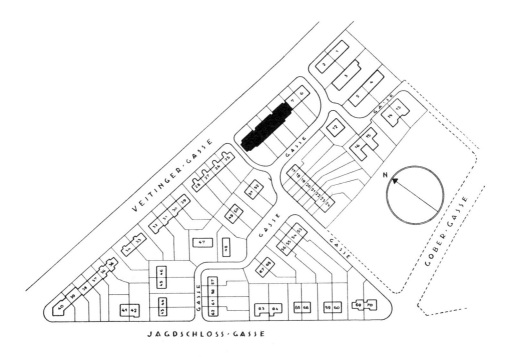

General site plan with Hoffmann's houses in black

1–5	Hugo Häring (Germany)
6–7	Richard Bauer
12	Josef Frank
13–14	Oskar Strnad
15–16	Anton Brenner
17–18	K. A. Bieber and O. Niedermoser
19–20	Walter Loos
21–22	Eugen Wachberger
23–24	Clemens Holzmeister
25–28	André Lurçat (France)
29–30	Walter Sobotka
31–32	Oskar Wlach
33–34	Julius Jirasek
35–36	Ernst Plischke
37–38	Josef Wenzel
39–40	Oswald Haerdtl
41–42	Ernst Lichtblau
43–44	Hugo Gorge
45–46	J. Groag
47	Richard Neutra (U.S.A.)
48	Hans Vetter
49–52	Adolf Loos
53–56	Gerrit Rietveld (Holland)
57–58	Max Fellerer
59–60	Otto Breuer
61–62	Grete Lihotzki Schütte
63–64	A. Grünberger (U.S.A.)
65–66	Josef F. Dex
67–68	Gabriel Guevrekian (France)
69–70	Helmut Wagner-Freynsheim

Preliminary elevation sketches

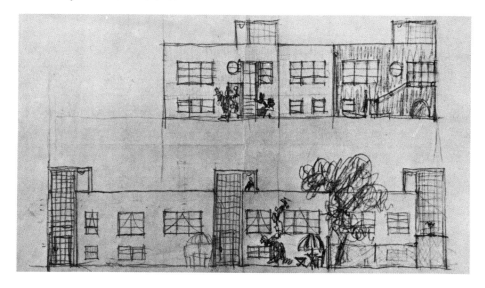

Street and garden elevations

Alternative plan types in black, with mirror-image plans in gray showing a different furniture arrangement

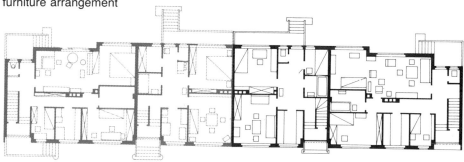

Hoffmann's duplex row housing with its compact planning was enormously successful, although the houses soon revealed some major technical imperfections. In the end, they came to cost more than traditional houses. The correspondent of *AC*, the magazine of GATEPAC, emphasized the independent character of Viennese architecture, but no one questioned why Adolf Loos had been excluded from the debate over suitable housing types. Instead they strongly praised the young architect Walter Loos, a distant relative, for his double-height housing of less than 30 square meters in area, as well as the houses of Hoffmann, which suggested all at once the manneristic character of houses by Rietveld, Häring, and Lurçat.

Hoffmann certainly did not pass up the opportunity to declare once again his lack of interest in this type, and focused his attention more on the overall architectural image than on the interiors fitted out by the Prague studios. The buildings of the Werkbundsiedlung thus posed a number of questions to the city of *Höfe*, among which was that of the possibility of resolving the housing crisis along the lines of the proposals of the avant-garde. While the work of Le Corbusier, Mies, and Gropius would diverge after this period, Hoffmann was still able to provide them with this lesson on style: that the language of the avant-garde could be adopted and transformed, using it exactly like any other language to "compose," only by working on a very high conceptual and professional level.

Facade with the glazed stair towers

Two views of the rear facade overlooking the garden just after construction

Exhibition catalogue

Street facade

Interior with furniture by Hoffmann

One of the entrances today

1930   Monument to Otto Wagner

Makartgasse 1, Vienna

In honor of the master who died in 1918, Hoffmann designed a monument which was at first placed in the courtyard of the Academy on the Schillerplatz. From among several possible designs—a lighthouse with a spiral ramp winding to the top, a vaguely Art Déco column with close-set planes, and a pyramidal obelisk like those he had so often used in the courtyards of his exhibition pavilions—Hoffmann finally chose a very conventional and Wagnerian shape, a simple granite pillar with the inscription: "Dem grossen Baukünstler Otto Wagner" (To the greatest architect, Otto Wagner), in letter forms taken directly from the Werkstätte. There was nothing more appropriate for the master of ambiguity and silence.

The inscription

The monument in the Schillerplatz

Sketches of the project

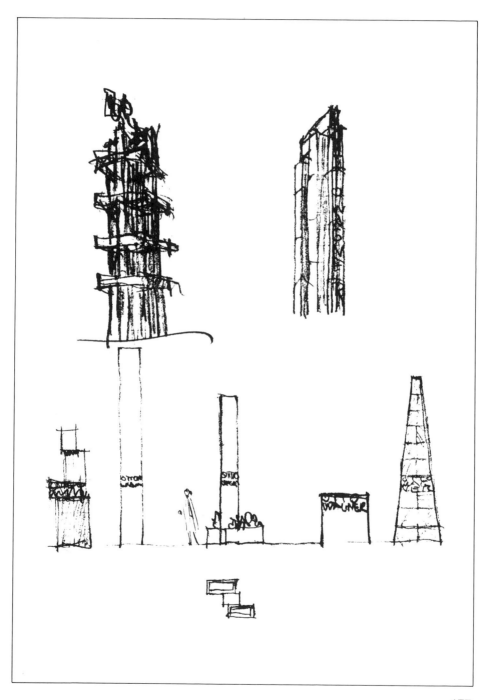

1930

Prototype for a Railroad Car for the Austrian Railways

In the biography he produced for the celebration in Vienna of Hoffmann's sixtieth birthday, Rochowanski records that this famous prototype was exceptionally successful. It was done at a time when Hoffmann enjoyed getting involved in every detail of his designs and was curious about every aspect of production.

Consciously ignoring technical difficulties, Hoffmann fitted out a standard car exactly as he would have done a room at the time of the Secession. Although the production of the cars, which was to have helped to revive the national railroad stock, was put aside because of the economic crisis, this prototype was examined again long afterwards, and was apparently considered even after World War II. Hoffmann knew how to solve a perpetual problem: how to provide maximum comfort in a minimum of space. For him, it was basically a matter of creating a temporary house.

Interior of the railroad car:
view down the corridor

Detail of window and wash basin

Details of the compartment

1929

Study for an Apartment Building for the City of Vienna

The heroic character of socialist Vienna generally inspired the architects of the city to adopt a style that was both symbolic and celebratory. In the Klosehof and Winarskyhof, Hoffmann too had demonstrated this inclination, although it was partly hidden beneath his obvious intention of bestowing a domestic character upon the housing.

Before turning to the project for the XIXth district, he evidently had time to consider the possibility of integrating the two tendencies popular at that time: the functional and the decorative. The risk was, as usual, that one would end up with a style resembling Art Nouveau.

The facades with their strongly defined profiles and sharp corners are clad in a precious material similar to that found in Adolf Loos's interiors, and on the flat roof, as large as a football field, the gazebo makes its amusing appearance for the last time.

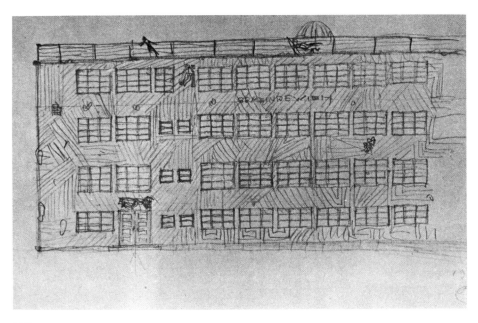

1927

Study for a
Terraced Housing Block

This is one of numerous designs halfway between fantasy and concrete proposal which Hoffmann made after his experiences with the Werkbundsiedlung. An unlikely Loosian nostalgia and iconographic evocations of the Palais Stoclet recur in this as in several other proposals.

The corners of the cornices obsessively frame this imaginative composition of built-up, terraced volumes, outlining volumes and facade planes in which windows—as many as the space allows—open without meaning, while an improbably long spiral of ivy wraps its way up the whole block.

1930–1932   Laxenburgerstrassehof

Laxenburgerstrasse 94, Vienna V

This is one of the last large public apartment blocks constructed within the city's building program. Subsequent developments were connected with the proposals of the Werkbund, while the socialist government became immobilized by the increasingly hostile international political situation and the economic crisis as well as by the internal opposition groups which subsequently brought about the tragic events of 1933.

Here, Hoffmann, pushing to an extreme his own repertory of formal solutions, closed the block on itself, giving the courtyard only one entrance. The impression of impenetrability is present still today, in spite of renovations and the fact that the exterior with its rhythmic courses of balconies has been tampered with. The main entrance is a "door" in the oldest meaning of the word, and the internal entrances to each part of the block open directly on the courtyard, as do windows which faintly recall those of Behrens in the Winarskyhof. The dimensions of the apartments are now sharply reduced, to between 48 and 60 square meters, with some one-room studio apartments on the top floor. The exterior was originally plastered white. The slate roof and strong shadows cast by the window perforations in the facade give the building a tense plasticity and a certain dramatic beauty.

Exterior corner of block

Plan and elevations

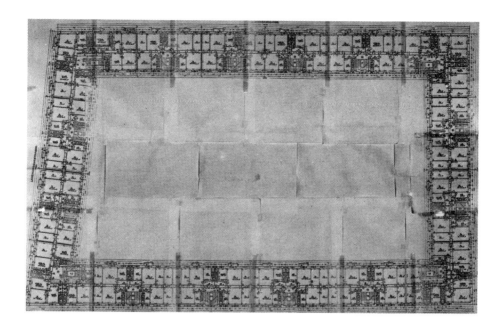

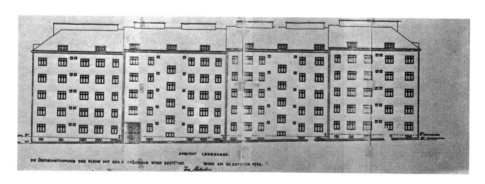

1932

Study for a Small Pavilion for the Wiener Werkstätte

The idea of a single pavilion or gazebo with no other function than to recall a happier period when all forms were possible appears together with similar proposals at about the time when the Wiener Werkstätte was finally dissolved. As one commentator has written, ". . . This man Hoffmann, who did not know how to balance his books and who had dissipated the patrimony of three wealthy men in the Wiener Werkstätte . . . was the only one who knew how to build pavilions. Sadly, what seemed to have been built to last forever was in fact only destined to survive for a brief moment."

1932

Study for a Housing Block

A more flexible rationalism, a defense of the ephemeral in architecture, and an avowed desire to resist the rigid canon of the International Style led Hoffmann to explore unusual hypotheses, including the possibility of making decoration a determining architectural element.

In this rationalist building, with the *fenêtres en longueur* of its large living rooms extending across the entire facade, there is no conflict in using the traditional Viennese roof in place of the flat one, nor in having a cellar instead of *pilotis.* The street facade is dissolved in a delicate Klimtian pink, as the watercolor drawing of the project reveals, and frescoed in a shade suggesting interiors and upholstered fabric. One is immediately reminded of Wagner's house on the Linke Wienzeile.

1934

Austrian Pavilion at the Venice Biennale

The Austrian experiments in Social Democracy ended abruptly in February 1934. From now on the political destiny of the republic would be similar to that of Nazi Germany. Many of the leading artists in Hoffmann's circle in Vienna quietly became associated with the right wing, and Hoffmann himself was consulted more than once by the official party organizations. Adolf Loos died in Kalzburg at the beginning of this year.

The Austrian pavilion in Venice, built in a climate of general retreat from festive architecture, is the last of Hoffman's works to be entirely designed by him after the final dissolution of the Wiener Werkstätte. Constructed of brick, it was finished in a great hurry and situated on the Rio dei Giardini next to the present Yugoslavian pavilion.

Light filtered down from the ceiling and was scattered along the walls of the interior rooms, which were divided by a modest porticoed gallery. The interior and exterior both speak a language harsh with the accents of protocol, a language which still clearly communicates its message: in 1934, emptiness and absence are the only choices possible.

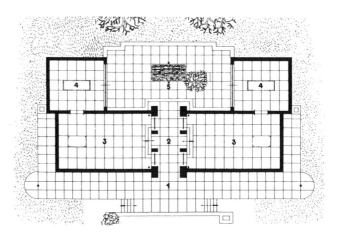

Plan

1 Entrance
2 Atrium
3 Exhibition halls
4 Sculpture galleries
5 Loggia and fountain

Project sketch of the rear loggia

Studies of the front facade

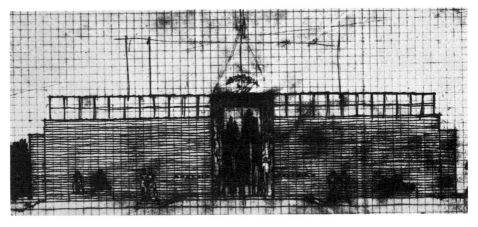

Austrian Pavilion at the Venice Biennale (continued)

Facade of the pavilion just after completion

Interior

1934   Contempora House

Rockland, New York

Paul Lester Wiener, architect and interior designer known for his collaboration with Bruno Paul on a studio for the applied arts (Contempora International Art Service), obtained Hoffmann's permission in 1930 to build a residence in Rockland, using one of the designs Hoffmann gave him after the dissolution of the Wiener Werkstätte.

    The finished work recalls Hoffman's "manner" more than his precise style. The rustic stone which Hoffmann had planned to use in clever contrast to the refinement of the details is here hidden beneath the uniform stucco of the International Style, and the entire building appears to have been translated into another language.

    No traces of the lessons Wiener had learned from Hoffmann may be seen in his later collaborative work with Niemeyer and Costa for the Brazilian pavilion at the 1938 New York World's Fair. The International Style was incapable of accepting the ideals and vocabulary which belonged to the "noble language" of architecture. Orthodox rationalism distanced itself from time-honored models and relegated them to a lost past.

Hoffmann's sketch for the west facade

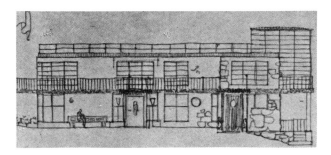

East facade of the house at Rockland, with the dining terrace

Biography

1870   Josef Hoffmann was born in Pirnitz, Moravia, on December 16th, the fourth son and namesake of the town burgomaster. The family, descended from travelers and merchants, had at the beginning of the century founded a spinning mill and was engaged in the production of hand-printed fabrics. Hoffmann's mother, Leopoldina, was an enthusiastic and talented musician, and she frequently visited the castle of Prince Collalto, whose art collection and gardens were among the most famous in Moravia.

1879   Josef, called "Pepo," enrolled in the state school at Iglau intending to pursue classical studies and take up a career in law. Seeing his poor performance, and noticing his interest in art and design, his parents subsequently enrolled him in the Institute of Arts and Crafts at Brno, which he left for one year to serve an apprenticeship at Würzburg in the military building division of the government.

1892   He enrolled at the Academy of Fine Arts in Vienna, under Carl von Hasenauer, collaborator of Gottfried Semper and designer of the Imperial Museums and Burgtheater. During this period Hoffmann frequented theatrical circles and also founded a society of poets.

1894   Otto Wagner, who three years earlier had published *Einige Skizzen,* was asked to replace Hasenauer at the Academy. Hoffmann was one of Wagner's most diligent followers.

Two years further into his studies, during Wagner's professorship, he founded the Society of Seven with Olbrich, Carl Otto Czeschka, Koloman Moser, Leo Kainradl, and others at the Café Sperl. This was a society of "friends of the arts," which, with Wagner's tacit approval, proceeded to expand the program of the school to the wider context of European artistic developments. Some months later, Olbrich, winner of the *prix de Rome,* left for Italy, and then went on to Tunisia and Egypt. He sent Hoffmann many letters with observations on the places and monuments he visited, and a strong similarity of interests between the two men was established.

1895   Hoffmann received his diploma and his project, "Forum Orbis – Insula Pacis" won him the *prix de Rome.* A few months later Hoffmann left for his own trip to Italy, a classical grand tour on a route similar to that which Goethe and other eighteenth- and nineteenth-century German travelers had taken. He visited Bolzano, Trent, Verona, Vicenza, Venice, Istria, Parenzo, and Volosca; then he went to Ancona, Florence, Rome, Naples, Capri, Pozzuoli, Amalfi, and Pompeii. During the trip he made over 200 sketches, some published in the same year in *Der Architekt,* as illustrations for an article entitled "Architecture of the Austrian Riviera."

1898   Thanks to Wagner's support and financing by Viennese businessmen, Moser, Klimt, Hoffmann, Olbrich, and Carl Moll established the *Vereinigung der bildenden Künstler Österreichs* (Society for Austrian Artists), better known as the Vienna Secession, for which

Olbrich built his famous building in the same year.

The group's magazine was established and first published in January, under the title *Ver Sacrum*. Among the various editors were Arno Holz, Richard Huch, Rudolf Jettmar, Dehmel, Rilke, Schaukal, Maeterlinck, and others.

On April 5th, the group's first exhibition opened in the hall of the Gartenbaugesellschaft on the Parking. Meunier, Giovanni Segantini, and Fernand Khnopff also participated. In November, Olbrich's building was completed, and Hoffmann carried out the decoration of the secretary's office.

1899 Olbrich, who had in the meantime distinguished himself as one of the most ambitious architects in Vienna (having already completed plans for the Stohr house, the tomb of the Klarwill family, the interiors of the villas Berl and Stift, the design for the Friedman house at Hinterbrühl, and the Bahr house), was asked by the Duke of Hessen in Darmstadt to come and build an artists' colony there, and Olbrich then effectively left the Vienna Secession.

1900 Felician Freiherr von Myrbach, director of the School of Arts and Crafts, invited Hoffmann to go to London where he made contact with the English circle and met Charles Rennie Mackintosh. *Das Interieur* published Hoffmann's first projects, while he, in the meantime, concentrated on designing furniture (for the Brix, Grün, and Wittgenstein houses, and the Apollo Store in Vienna). Some of his pieces, among them the famous "musical furniture" were produced.

1900 was also the year of the VIIIth Exhibition of the Secession. On this occasion, under Hoffmann's initiative, examples of all European craftsmanship were on show in Vienna for the first time, from Ashbee's Guild of Handicraft and Mackintosh-Macdonald's furniture to that of van de Velde and the *Maison moderne* of Paris.

1902 Fritz Wärndorfer, back from a trip to England where he had met Mackintosh, financed the founding of the workshop for the production of objects designed by the Secession. This would develop into the Wiener Werkstätte, for which Hoffmann drew up bylaws and a comprehensive program. The direction of the Werkstätte was entrusted to Hoffmann and Kolo Moser, with Wärndorfer assuming an administrative role. At this time, a register of inventors' and designers' marks was also established.

With Olbrich's departure to Darmstadt, the commission for construction of a group of villas on the Hohe Warte, a suburb of Vienna, fell to Hoffmann. His clients, well known in artistic and professional circles, were closely connected to the Secession and the Werkstätte, and included Moll, Henneberg, Moser, Spitzer, and others. The completion of the villas was to provide Hoffmann with a major reputation: plans and photographs were published in *Das Interieur* and other journals. In 1902, the widely acclaimed masterpiece of this period, the Klinger room for the XIVth Exhibition of the Secession, on which Klimt and Rudolf Jettmar also collaborated, was completed, as well as a small church in Hohenburg.

1903 The Wiener Werkstätte moved to Neustiftgasse 32. The production was already on an international scale and had reached one hundred items. Among the main collaborators of this period were Czeschka and Eduard Wimmer.

Vincent van Gogh's first painting to be seen in Austria, the *View Towards Auvers-sur-Oise,* made a strong impression on the Secession members. On the encouragement of Hoffmann and Moser, Klimt departed for Ravenna, accompanied by the painter Lenz, and visited Florence, Desenzano, and Venice.

1904   Plan for the Sanatorium at Purkersdorf, near Vienna. Hoffmann and Kolo Moser created the interiors, also designing all the technical and decorative details of the building. Hoffmann met the Belgian couple Adolphe Stoclet and Suzanne Stevens (the future aunt of Mallet-Stevens) in Carl Moll's house. The Stoclet house was first conceived for the Hohe Warte on the site where the Villa Ast was later built. Otto Wagner built the Postsparkasse in Vienna; Berlage the Stock Exchange in Amsterdam.

1905   Klimt, Hoffmann, Moll, Moser, Wagner, and Richard Luksch left the Secession. The Stoclets returned to Brussels, finalizing the contract for their house. Hoffmann traveled to Belgium and Flanders, developing his collaboration with Kolo Moser, who at this time designed the stained glass windows of Wagner's church at Steinhof.

1906   Work began on the Palais Stoclet, entrusted by Hoffmann to the architect Emil Gerzabek. The Kohn firm began to produce the famous curved chair for the sanatorium at Purkersdorf. Klimt, Michael Powolny, Czeschka, Berthdd Löffler, the Luksch couple, Lady Schleiss-Simandl, Moser, Forstner, Franz Metzner, and Georges Minne, associated with Hoffmann in the design of the Palais Stoclet.

1907   Hoffmann offered work to Le Corbusier, who passed through Vienna after his first trip to Italy. Meanwhile, work on the Palais Stoclet proceeded in Brussels under the direction of Gerzabek. Hoffmann was intensely involved in design and planning in Vienna: the Villa Wittgenstein near Hohenberg, the Villa Hochstätter, and the completion of the first shop for the Wiener Werkstätte in the Graben. This led to the formation of a separate studio for painting. L. Hevesi published the account *Acht Jahre Sezession* (Eight years of the Secession). In Germany, the Deutscher Werkbund was established.

1908   Olbrich died in Düsseldorf. In Zurich, Maillart built the Lagerhaus in reinforced concrete with mushroom columns.

In Vienna, a major new *Kunstschau* exhibition was in preparation. The capital was scandalized by Klimt's *Danae,* which would later be bought by Eduard Ast.

1909   Gustav Klimt executed the mosaics for the dining room of the Stoclets: " . . . faint figures like memories," wrote Rochowanski. Hoffmann designed the interior decoration for a new apartment for Sonia Knips, and became involved in the design of women's fashions.

De Chirico, who in the meantime had come to know the painter Max Klinger, painted his *Lotta tra i Lapiti e i Centauri.* Hoffmann met Paul Poiret, who had been invited by the Werkstätte.

1910   Design and construction of the Austrian Pavilion in Rome for the celebration of the fiftieth anniversary of the Kingdom of Italy. Debate in the Austrian press over Hoffmann's "new path" (in *Die Kunst, Zeitschrift für Bildende Kunst,* etc.). Design and commencement of construction of the Villa Ast on the Hohe Warte. In Brussels, the Palais Stoclet was completed. Adolf Loos was engaged in the project for the house on the Michaelerplatz. Among the unrealized projects which Hoffmann began in this period was the theater for Kapfenberg.

1912　Hoffman designed the residential village of Kaasgraben on the western periphery of Vienna. These six villas, still well preserved today, are an attempt to translate earlier solutions to buildings of a smaller scale. There are interesting experiments with basic construction materials: concrete and brick.

1913　Fritz Wärndorfer, the first financier of the Wiener Werkstätte, left Austria for the United States. He was replaced by the banker Otto Primavesi, who had engaged Hoffmann to build an imposing villa for entertainment purposes on Gloriettegasse in Schönbrunn, without any regard to expense.
Friedrich Achleitner recalls of this period: "Hoffmann's indefatigable preoccupation with formal concerns concealed a deep aversion for repetition, so much so that he did not participate in discussions on standardization (the controversy between Muthesius and van de Velde). It has been said of him that if a client began to lose interest in a particular design, Hoffmann would immediately offer him another more beautiful one. Although this anecdote may have been invented, the story is very characteristic of Hoffmann and of the

spirit of the Wiener Werkstätte in general. At the same time, in this attitude may be discerned a very specific characteristic of the Wiener Werkstätte: its production was not based on economic criteria."

1914　Hoffmann's work began to point the way towards what would later be called his neoclassical style, designing the Austrian pavilion at the Cologne Fair in collaboration with Anton Hanak and Oskar Strnad.
Archduke Ferdinand was assassinated at Sarajevo and the First World War broke out. The Wiener Werkstätte was heavily affected by the general economic crisis. In Italy, Antonio Sant'Elia drew up the *Manifesto of Futurist Architecture.*

1915–18　Great activity in the area of interior design: Hoffmann was invited to put on one-man shows in Stockholm and Copenhagen. In April 1918, Otto Wagner died. In the same year Klimt, Moser, Schiele, and Peter Altenberg also died. On November 11, 1918, the Republic was proclaimed and, at dawn, the new red and white flag was raised in Parliament.

1918–21　Intense design activity: in the studios of the Wiener Werkstätte the unique figure of Dagobert Peche became increasingly dominant. He almost overshadowed Hoffmann. Peche's work became closely identified with that of the Werkstätte in its attempted resistance to industrialism at this point, its moment of greatest fame as well as the beginning of the end of the whole movement. In 1916, in *Österreichische Werkkultur,* a volume published by the Austrian Werkbund, Max Eisler had written: "…Austrian applied art has shown its strength first in craftsmanship and secondly as an industry. The exact reverse is true of the German applied arts. Although this is a result of economic conditions, it is certainly an advantage as far as artistic quality is concerned."

1922–24 Design and construction of the country house of Councillor Ast on Lake Velden in Carinzia, based on the Knips house in Vienna. Peter Behrens was named professor at the Academy in Vienna. Hoffmann moved his residence to Schleifmühlgasse 7. He obtained from the progressive new administration the commission for a large apartment block, the Klosehof, and, with Behrens, Strnad, and others, also the commission for the Winarskyhof.

1925 The Exhibition of Decorative Arts took place in Paris. Hoffmann, together with Behrens and a group including Josef Frank and Strnad, constructed the Austrian pavilion in the very center of the exhibition. Despite the presence of the L'Esprit Nouveau pavilion and of the buildings of Melnikov and Tony Garnier, the impact of Hoffmann's work on the modern architects was enormous. His avowed inclination towards the decorative, which was obvious on this occasion, caused speculation about a possible neo-baroque revival.

1928 On July 26th at the second session of the congress of the first CIAM, held at the castle of La Sarraz, the debate opened with the proposal of names for participation in the International Committee for the Solution of the Problems of Modern Architecture, CIRPAC. This group was charged with promoting contacts between the organizational arm of the congresses and governmental organizations. The Austrian Gubler was strongly opposed to the nomination of Hoffmann, whom Le Corbusier had initially proposed, citing Hoffmann's "untenable" position in the international movement. "He is neither modern nor scholarly," he said. In the debate which followed, despite the full support of Frank and Victor Bourgeois, it was decided by all, with the sole opposition of Jean Lurçat, to exclude Hoffmann as well as Wright from the committee. Bourgeois later commented upon the decision: " . . . in five years the younger architects will probably be even more severe towards us than we have been towards Hoffmann."

1928–29 These were years in which Hoffmann became interested in large-scale projects. He sent plans to the city administration for the reconstruction of entire parts of the city: the famous project for the Palace of Art and Culture on the Karlsplatz, the restructuring of the Stadtpark, and the creation of a new exhibition area and new docks on the Danube.
Hoffmann was named State Commissioner for National and International Competitions, joining the jury which was to judge the competition entries for the new Palace of Nations in Geneva. He openly favored Le Corbusier's project, especially after the Swiss architect's polemic. Hoffmann also participated in the conferences on cultural activity in the Volkschule (public school system).

1930 Hoffmann was elected vice-president of the Austrian section of the Werkbund. The Werkbund congress held in Vienna was celebrated with an exhibition aiming to interest the whole city through a series of housing projects based on the typological experiments discussed at the various international congresses. Hoffmann worked collaboratively with Frank, Strnad, and Walter Sobotka. For this occasion the Werkbund published a book commemorating Hoffmann's work. It included articles by Asplund, Behrens, Berlage, Le Corbusier, Frank, Gropius, Papini, Poelzig, and others.

Gio Ponti recalls of Hoffmann at this time: "Politics never interested him. He loved Voltaire, Anatole France, and, most of all, Chinese literature, as well as everything children said and did. He had two wives, both beautiful and blonde. His friends knew little of his private life, only that there was a wife and a son they might see by chance after years of not seeing them. As for the son, he would say to his father: 'You know, yesterday I got married and tomorrow we will leave for New York.' . . . A short trip. He refused chairs at architecture schools in Germany and America. He had his roots in Vienna and in that Austria which, only a few kilometers from the city, is rural, natural, and silent . . . "

1932   Hoffmann participated in the definition of the Werkbund program for the building of a "model housing quarter" in Vienna and realized his famous duplex row houses there which were much discussed because the costs exceeded all expectations. The polemics that this stirred up forced Hoffmann to resign from the organization. The president, Hermann Neubacher (future mayor of Vienna under the Nazis), effectively withdrew his support and, solely through the efforts of Josef Frank, formed a new executive whose president was Clemens Holzmeister. Behrens and Hoffmann became vice-presidents. Jews and left-wing sympathizers were excluded from the organization. Frank then emigrated to Switzerland.

1934   Hoffmann designed and constructed the Austrian Pavilion for the Venice Biennale. From then on, his activities were increasingly confined to studies and projects, and he was only occasionally consulted by the National Socialist Party. Clemens Holzmeister became State Commissioner for Art under the Dollfuss government and an advisor on matters concerning art. Vienna was now in the hands of strong conservative forces and the Neuer Werkbund, a "purified" organization, was founded. Hoffmann organized the exhibition "Free Craftsmanship" with the enthusiasm of pro-industrialists. Critics openly accused him of having been a poor administrator of the Werkstätte's resources and to have more or less brought about its collapse. Achleitner wrote: "Vien-nese society finally seemed to have been put in order."

1954   The first biographical study of Hoffmann and his work was published on his eightieth birthday, and the festivities surrounding this were organized by the Ministry of Public Education in Vienna.

1956   Hoffmann died on May 15th in his house on Salesianergasse 33 in Vienna.

List of Major Works[1]

Page references are given for projects illustrated in this book.

Hoffmann house in Pirnitz, Moravia
Cafe Graben, Vienna

1912–1913 Offices of the Poldihütte firm, Vienna

1912–1914 Colony of villas in Kaasgraben, Vienna (*page 102*): Villa Wellesz, Villa Botstiber, Villa Vetter, Villa Herzka, Villa Küper, Villa Drucker
Renovation of the Villa Koller, Vienna
Villa Bernatzik, Vienna
Exhibition installation at the Museum of Art and Industry, Vienna
Tomb for the Förster family, Vienna

1913–1915 Villa Primavesi, Vienna (*page 106*)

1914 Country house for the Primavesi family, Winkelsdorf, Moravia (*page 125*)
Pavilion for the Leipzig publishing exhibition (*page 124*)
Austrian Pavilion at the German Werkbund exhibition, Cologne (*page 122*)
Renovation of the Primavesi Bank, Olmütz

1915 Furnishings for the Gödl-Olajossy house, Linz

1915–1916 Furnishings for the Böhler house, Munich

1916 Apartment for Anton Knips, Gumpendorferstrasse 15, Vienna
Apartment for Berta Zuckerkandl, Oppolzergasse 6, Vienna
Tomb for the Strosz family, Vienna

1916–1917 Apartment for Paul Wittgenstein, Friedrich-Schmidt-Platz 6, Vienna
Wiener Werkstätte store, Kärntnerstrasse, Vienna
Factory for Dr. Wacker, Burghausen
Studio for Heinrich Böhler, Schwarzenbergpalais, Vienna

1917 Project for a Palace of Culture and Thought, Stockholm (*page 126*)
Wiener Werkstätte store, Marienbad, Bohemia

1917–1918 Apartment for Erwin Böhler, Parkring 4, Vienna
Project for the city hall of Ortelsburg

1917–1919 Modifications to the *Poldihütte* plant, Kladno, Bohemia

1918 Primavesi apartment, Teggethofstrasse 4, Vienna
Apartment for Dr. Berstel, Vienna-Neustad
Tomb for the Steiner family, Vienna
Austrian Pavilion at the Leipzig Fair
Project for the Pazzani house, Vienna

1919 Project for the Anton Knips house, Vienna
Tomb for the Hamberger family, Freudenthal, Silesia

1919–1920 Tomb for the Knips family, Vienna

1920 Project for a country house for the Pazzani family, Admont
Rehabilitation of the sanatorium in Bad Ullersdorf
Project for a bank in Novisad
Project for a restaurant and a cafe in Laxenburg

1920–1921 Bernatzik apartment adjoining the Villa Ast, Hohe Warte, Vienna

1920–1922 Project for interiors for the house of Dr. Pazzani, Pichl, Styria
Design and construction of the Berl house (sometimes called Berlin), Freudenthal, Silesia
Grohmann house, Würbenthal, Silesia

1921 Furnishings for a two-room apartment for Ernst Gallia, Einwanggasse 15, Vienna
Project for a hotel in Zagreb
Memorial for the war dead, Pirnitz, Moravia

1922 Apartment for Dr. Kuno Grohmann, Pochmühl, Silesia

1922–1923 Apartment for Dr. Robert Baru, Schönbrunnergasse 217, Vienna
Casa Dunckel, Budapest

1. In the dating of Hoffmann's works there tends to be some variation and inexactness, in all probability due to the fact that it has often been quite difficult to obtain the original material. Certain documents in the Bildarchiv in Vienna, for example, are catalogued under years in which the projects could not have been executed; there are also notable variations among the contemporary authors. For the most part we have followed the official catalogue of the exhibition of Hoffmann's work held in Vienna in 1980 (*Josef Hoffmann: Architect and Designer 1870–1956*. Vienna and New York: Galerie Metropol, 1980), except in those cases where legitimate doubts have arisen.

Pictorial and Bibliographical Sources

Akademie der bildenden Künste, Vienna
Bildarchiv der Österreichischen Nationalbibliothek, Vienna
Giuliano Gresleri, Bologna
Paolo Gresleri, Bologna
Museum Moderner Kunst, Vienna
Österreichisches Museum für angewandte Kunst, Vienna
Umberto Tasca, Bologna

The description of some of the drawings and designs has been based on the following books and articles, which may serve as an initial bibliography:

Ver Sacrum I (1898), no. 5–6; IV (1901), no. 12.
Der Architekt VII (1901).
Moderne Bauformen XII (1913); XIII (1914).
Josef Hoffmann zum Sechzigsten Geburtstag. Vienna: Österreichischer Werkbund, 1930.
Architectural Record, July 1935.
Domus 93 (Sept. 1935).
E. F. Sekler. "The Stoclet House by Josef Hoffmann." In *Essays in the History of Architecture Presented to Rudolf Wittkower*. London: Phaidon, 1967.
L'Arte Moderna III, no. 19. Milan: Fratelli Fabbri, 1967.
Artisti austriaci a Roma dal Barocco alla Secessione. Rome: Istituto austriaco di cultura, 1972.
G. Feuerstein. *Wien heute und gestern*. Fremdenverkehrsverband für Wien, 1974.
Wiener Architektur 1860–1930 in Zeichnungen. Stuttgart: Verlag Gerd Hatje, 1979.
D. Müller. *Klassiker des modernen Möbeldesign*. Munich: Keyser, 1980.
Manfredo Tafuri, ed. *Vienna Rossa*. Milan: Electa, 1980.
Moderne Vergangenheit: Wien 1800–1900. Vienna: Gesellschaft bildender Künstler Österreichs, 1981.
Josef Hoffmann: Architect and Designer 1876–1956. Vienna and New York: Galeria Metropol, 1981.

See also Eduard Sekler's major monograph on Hoffman's work, published since the Italian edition of this book:
Eduard F. Sekler. *Josef Hoffmann: Das Architektonische Werk*. Vienna: Residenz Verlag, 1982.